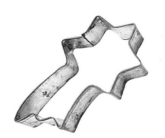

Over 100 delicious recipes

Christmas

Cookies - Cakes - Breads

Patrik Jaros

Contents

Introduction

Who can resist the spicy-sweet smell of freshly baked Christmas cookies? The word "calorie" vanishes from our brain as soon as the oven door opens and we can smell the delicious flavours of cinnamon, cardamom, cloves, orange peel and freshly baked dough. It's like magic – even if you don't have a sweet tooth, you just have to take a nibble.

Most people cannot resist the urge to bake their own Christmas goodies. Even after insisting all year long that this year there will be no cookie-baking, as soon as Advent time approaches we all catch baking fever. We study recipe books and search out Granny's old hand-written recipes. There is hardly any family who does not own a true treasure of family recipes for their own delicious Christmas treats. Whether it's gingerbread bear paws, vanilla crescents or coconut kisses, every family has their own traditional recipe for the truly best tasting cookies. Nevertheless, year after year every

amateur pastry chef is looking for new recipes to spice up the cookie tray and make it even more tempting. We have rummaged through recipe books of foreign countries for you.

Let us surprise you with the sweets of the Christmas season in Germany, Austria, Switzerland, Italy and France as well as Great Britain, the United States and Scandinavia. We'll tell you about the typical sweets from these countries.

And of course we did not forget all the classic cookies. Just in case you cannot find your trusted, handed-down family recipe – why not try our version of vanilla crescents, cinnamon stars, gingerbread, etc.? For the restless baking fanatic there is a large selection of the best Christmas stollen recipes – one juicier and more flavourful than the last.

The same holds true for almonds, nuts, seeds and flaked coconut. If this is where you are trying to save money, you are saving in the wrong place. Also with regard to butter and eggs – use only fresh products, and make it worth your time and effort. You do want to get praise and recognition for your creations, don't you?

Baking at Christmas time is a special kind of joy. Children big and small love nothing more than kneading dough, rolling it out, cutting out cookies, placing the cookies on the tray and nibbling dough again and again. And if thick snow flakes are fluttering down from the sky outside your window, the Christmas baking fun is just perfect. Have a great time!

We describe all the basic doughs step by step, so nothing can go wrong! Even kitchen novices can easily follow these procedures and will surprise their loved ones with their baked goods.

Since you want your small sweet creations to look beautiful, one entire chapter is exclusively dedicated to decorating. Here we teach you how to spin sugar, what to watch out for so your chocolate coating turns out glossy and what kind of decorating accessories you can purchase in the stores. Anything that looks so tempting must taste just as delicious. The secret to flavourful Christmas cookies is not only the right recipes but most of all the right ingredients. All your hard work can be wasted if you use last year's spices for example which have lost all their flavour or if your candied orange and citron peels were bought in a super market with a poor selection and are bone dry.

Kitchen Tools
& Baking Moulds

Wire rack

An absolute necessity for Christmas baking. It is used to cool cookies after baking. Cookies that have been coated with chocolate or icing can drip-dry well on the rack.

Butter dish and brush

This is needed to brush cookies before and during baking or to brush Christmas stollen and printen.

Hand blender

A necessity in every household, it is used to whisk doughs, beat egg whites or cream butter.

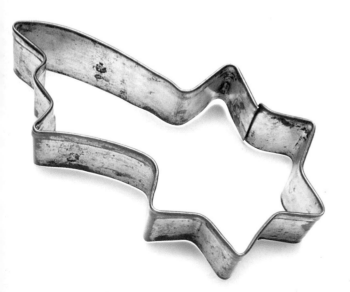

Cookie cutters

Cookie cutters come in different shapes and are a must for Christmas baking. If you are cutting dough, dip the cookie cutter into flour first or dip it into hot water for cutting jelly.

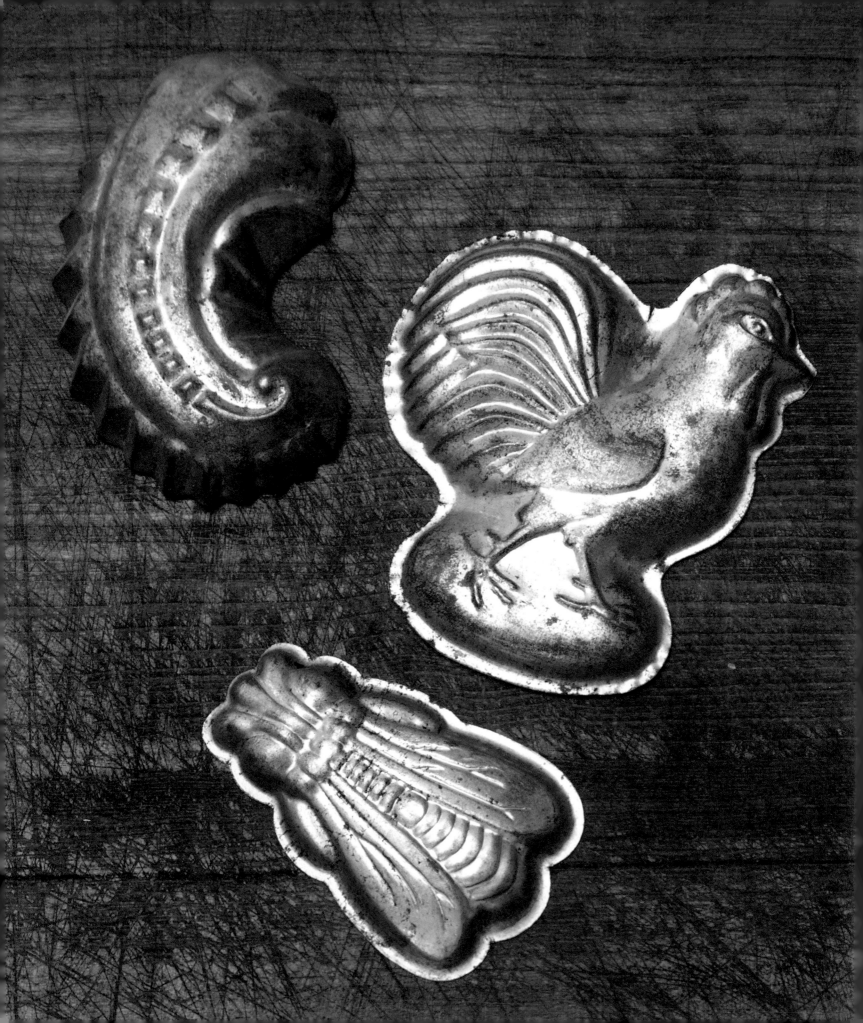

Rolling pin imprinted with different patterns

Used for rolling out dough with a pattern. This way you'll easily create an interesting surface on your cookies.

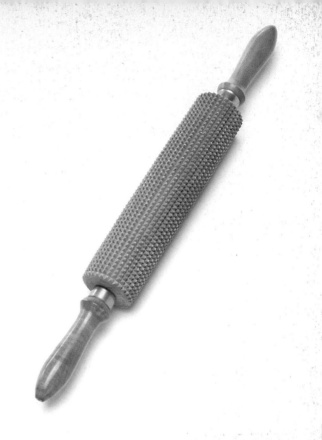

Decorative baking moulds

Rolled out dough is pressed into these moulds. After baking, turn moulds out onto wire rack. Children especially enjoy baking with these fun moulds.

Waffle iron

Fresh baked waffles sprinkled with cinnamon sugar taste especially delicious during the cold Christmas season. A coated waffle iron is preferred, since dough loosens easier and you need very little oil. Waffles taste great plain, but you can also serve them with hot cherries and whipped cream, hot chocolate and ice cream or a punch sauce.

Basic Doughs
& Spice Mixtures

Gingerbread Dough

240 g/8 1/2 oz honey

160 g/5 oz sugar

200 g/7 oz rye flour (type 1150)

400 g/14 oz wheat flour
    (type 1050)

2 whole eggs

4 egg yolks

160 g/5 oz unsalted butter

16 g/3/4 oz baking soda

30 g/1 oz gingerbread
    spice - see page 26

This dough is very suitable for quickly building a gingerbread house.

Mix honey and sugar together and heat in the top of a double boiler to about 60 °C (110 °F) until all sugar crystals have dissolved. Remove from heat and allow to cool to room temperature. It is best to use a fairly liquid honey with a high water percentage. Add rye and wheat flours, whole egg and egg yolks and knead into a dough. Add butter, small pieces at a time. Finally work baking soda and spices into the dough and refrigerate overnight. Preheat oven to 170 °C (325 °F), Gas mark 3. Roll dough to 8 mm (1/8 in) thickness and cut as desired. Thinly brush with milk and bake for about 15 to 18 minutes. After baking, brush with milk, dextrin glaze or spun sugar icing, depending on use.

Gingerbread – Aged Dough

800 g/1 lb 12 oz honey

300 g/10,5 oz sugar

200 ml/7 fl oz water

75 g/3 oz invert sugar
    or liquid glucose

1.5 kg/3 lb 5 oz wheat
    flour (type 1050)

750 g/1 lb 10 oz rye flour
    (type 1150)

Spice dough:

150 g/5 oz sugar

150 ml/5 fl oz water

225 g/8 oz flour

50 g/2 oz gingerbread
    spice - see page 26

A pinch of salt

Peel of 1/2 organically grown
    lemon

Extract of 1 vanilla bean

Leavening agents:

20 g/3/4 oz bakers'
    ammonia

17 g/3/4 oz potash

Some water and egg white

Combine honey, sugar, water and invert sugar (or liquid glucose) and heat in top of a double boiler to about 60 °C (110 °F) until all sugar crystals have dissolved. Remove from heat and allow to cool to room temperature. Add rye and wheat flours and thoroughly knead dough. Wrap in cling-film and allow to rest in a cool room for at least 6 weeks. It is important that there are no temperature changes in the room.

To prepare gingerbread dough, first prepare spice dough by kneading all its ingredients together. Then knead together with aged dough. Mix the leavening agents separately - stir bakers' ammonia into water and potash into egg white - and knead into dough one after the other. It is best to perform a baking test before rolling out dough. Preheat oven to 170 °C (325 °F), Gas mark 3. Roll dough to 8 mm (1/8 in) thickness and cut as desired with a knife or cookie cutters. Thinly brush with milk and bake for about 15-18 minutes. After baking brush with milk, dextrin glaze or spun sugar icing, depending on use.

Honey-Spice Dough

The difference between gingerbread dough and honey-spice dough is that honey-spice dough is sweetened exclusively with honey.

Heat honey in top of a double boiler to about 60 °C (110 °F) until all sugar crystals have dissolved. Remove from heat and allow to cool to room temperature. Add rye and wheat flours and work into a dough. Knead aged dough well, wrap in cling-film and allow to rest in a cool room for at least 6 weeks. It is important that there are no temperature changes in the room. In the old days, the dough matured in thick wooden barrels. Today plastic tubs are used. Pastry makers used to prepare the aged Christmas dough right after Easter. For the preparation of the honey spice dough, first knead honey dough spices into dough. Afterwards mix the leavening agents separately - stir bakers' ammonia into water and potash into egg white - and knead into dough one after the other. Perform a baking test before rolling out the dough.

Preheat oven to 175 °C (330 °F), Gas mark 4 . Roll dough to 8 mm (1/8 in) thickness and cut as desired with a knife or cookie cutters. Thinly brush with milk and bake for about 15-18 minutes. After baking brush with milk, dextrin glaze or spun sugar icing depending on use.

1 kg/2 1/4 lb honey
500 g/1 lb 2 oz wheat
   flour (type 1050)
500 g/1 lb 2 oz rye flour
   (type 1150)
<u>**Spices:**</u>
50 g/2 oz gingerbread
   spice - see page 26
A pinch of salt
Peel of 1/2 organically grown
   lemon
Extract of 1 vanilla bean
<u>**Leavening agents:**</u>
20 g/3/4 oz bakers'
   ammonia
17 g/3/4 oz potash
Some water and egg white

Honey-Spice Glaze

Roast cornstarch in oven until dark brown and allow to cool. Pass through a fine-mesh sieve.

Stir about 50 g (1/2 cup) of starch together with about 200 ml (1 cup) cold water. Bring to a boil once. Coat hot honey-spice and gingerbread doughs with this glaze after baking. This glaze is also called dextrin glaze.

100 g/4 oz potato starch
About 200 ml/7 fl oz water

Shortbread Dough

400 g/14 oz flour (type 405)

200 g/7 oz cold unsalted butter

100 g/4 oz sugar

1-2 eggs, depending upon size

Extract of 1/2 vanilla bean

A pinch of organically grown lemon peel

A pinch of salt

Note:
The most common mistake when preparing short dough is to knead the dough too long. This will turn the dough tough and make it look dirty, and the cookies will turn brittle, not short as desired.

It is also important that all the ingredients are very cold and that the dough is prepared quickly.

Sift flour onto work surface and distribute cold butter in little pieces over flour. Add sugar, vanilla extract, lemon peel and salt and knead with cold hands until butter combines with other ingredients. Quickly work in eggs. Shape into a ball or a rectangle, wrap in cling-film and refrigerate for at least one hour.

Gingerbread Spice

100 g/4 oz cinnamon, sticks or ground

75 g/3 oz cloves, whole or ground

50 g/2 oz nutmeg, nut or ground

75 g/3 oz dried ginger, in one piece or ground

125 g/4 1/2 oz fennel seeds, whole or ground

125 g/4 1/2 oz coriander seeds, whole or ground

125 g/4 1/2 oz anise, whole or ground.

Either combine pulverised spices or finely crush and mix with vegetable chopper. About 25 g/1 oz (2 tbsp) spice mixture is needed for 1 kg/2 lb 12 oz dough.

Speculatius Spice

125 g/4 1/2 oz cinnamon sticks

10 g/1/2 oz mace

10 g/1/2 oz coriander seeds

20 g/3/4 oz cardamom capsules

25 g/1 oz pimento

6 vanilla beans

Crush all ingredients with vegetable chopper. Vanilla beans have to dry overnight. It is best to use scraped out vanilla beans where the extract has already been used for other preparations.

Honey-Dough Spice

50 g/2 oz cinnamon, sticks or ground

10 g/1/2 oz cloves, whole or ground

180g/6 oz coriander seeds, whole or ground

10 g/1/2 oz pimento corns, whole or ground

50 g/2 oz anise, whole or ground

5 g/1/4 oz nutmeg, nut or ground

Either combine pulverised spices or finely crush and mix with vegetable chopper. About 25 g/1 oz (2 tbsp) spice mixture is needed for 1 kg/2 lb 12 oz dough.

Elisen Gingerbread Spice

200 g/7 oz cinnamon sticks

30 g/1 oz cloves

20 g/3/4 oz cardamom capsules

30 g/1 oz pimento

6 vanilla beans

Crush all ingredients with vegetable chopper. Vanilla beans have to dry overnight. It is best to use scraped out vanilla beans where the extract has already been used for other preparations.

Star Anise

Star anise has an intense smell and flavour similar to anise. It is mainly used to flavour molasses. We know the taste of star anisette best from hot spiced wine

Lemon Peel

Thoroughly clean organically grown lemons with hot water and pat dry with a kitchen towel. Grate off only the yellow peel with a very fine kitchen grater. Combine 50 g (2 oz) lemon peel and 50 g (2 oz) sugar and keep in an airtight jar. It keeps well for a few months and the sugar preserves the flavour.

Ginger

Ginger can be purchased candied, ground or fresh. It has a very intense flavour and fresh ginger is quite hot. Therefore ginger should be used sparsely for baking. Candied ginger makes a great decoration for cookies or Christmas cakes.

Candied Citrus Peel

Candied citrus peel, also called candied lemon peel, is the candied peel of a certain lemon type with an especially flavourful peel. Candied citrus peel is available already finely diced and packaged. But, whole candied lemon peel has a richer flavour and better quality. Fresh candied citrus peel is soft and smells zesty.

Candied Orange Peel

Candied orange peel is the candied peel of organic bitter oranges also called bigarades. Candied orange peel is available already finely diced and packaged. But, whole candied orange peel has a richer flavour and better quality. Candied orange peel is one of the most important ingredients of stollen – therefore you should purchase only best quality.

Cloves

These dried buds of the clove tree can be purchased ground or whole. Cloves belong to the basic spices for different gingerbread and honey spice doughs. Be careful with the dosage, since cloves are strongly flavourtic and have a very intense fragrance. It is best to grind cloves yourself with a small mortar and pestle. Be very careful when measuring freshly ground cloves.

Sultanas

Sultanas are seedless and slightly bigger than raisins. They are also usually softer and fluffier than raisins. Sultanas are usually treated with sulphur dioxide for preservation, which turns them lighter in colour. If a recipe requires soaked sultanas, use warm black tea for best results.

Almonds

Almonds can be purchased whole, peeled or unpeeled, sliced or chopped. If you want to peel almonds yourself, place them into boiling water for 10 seconds. Rinse under cold water and remove brown peel from kernels.

Cinnamon

Cinnamon is certainly one of the most important Christmas spices and can be purchased as sticks from Ceylon or ground from China. For Christmas cookies one mainly uses ground cinnamon. Place a stick of cinnamon in a cup and cover with black tea. This is a wonderful alternative to hot spiced wine especially for children.

Brown Sugar

Brown sugar caramelises only lightly and is manufactured from a special molasses syrup. Its caramel and brown colours intensify the flavour. Brown sugar is used especially in dark doughs and gingerbread.

Coarse Sugar

Coarse sugar is mainly used for sprinkling over cookies. It turns cookies nice and crisp.

Confectioners' sugar

Mainly used for decoration. In Great Britain and the United States it is also known as **icing sugar**.

Sugar Pearls

Children especially love to decorate cookies with sugar pearls. Sprinkle pearls randomly onto fresh icing or arrange in different patterns onto the freshly covered cookies. Plain shortbread biscuits are turned into irresistible treats for young and older children when covered with coloured sugar pearls. Children also just love to decorate with these coloured sweets.

Pistachio Nuts

Pistachio nuts are the small, light green fruits of the pistachio tree. They not only look very decorative, they also taste great, almost sweet and very flavourful. Don't store them for very long. Pistachio paste is used to make fillings or cremes. Halved or chopped, the nuts can be used to decorate cookies, biscuits or tarts.

Flaked Coconut

Flaked coconut always adds an exotic touch to everything. Coconut kisses are a must on every Christmas cookie plate. A special treat: brush warm cookies with ginger jelly and dredge in lightly roasted, flaked coconut.

Bakers' Ammonia (Hartshorn), Potash & Co.

Bakers' ammonia is a leavening agent for height. It is also used to help biscuits rise. Bakers' ammonia needs to be dissolved in milk or water before it is mixed with dough.

Potash is a leavening agent for width. It is therefore solely used if you want your baked goods to expand sideways.

Potash cannot be added to gingerbread dough by itself. It needs to be dissolved first. Dissolved in water, it quickly loses its effect, therefore it is advisable to dissolve potash in beaten egg white.

In addition, potash reacts to acid. Allow gingerbread dough enough time to rise, because over time flour starts to ferment slightly and acid will form. This increases the effectiveness of the potash. In earlier times, gingerbread dough was already prepared at Easter for baking in late summer. Today one speeds up the fermenting process by adding sourdough, especially in the gingerbread industry.

Both potash and bakers' ammonia should only be combined with gingerbread dough after it has cooled to room temperature. Heat will ruin their effect.

Flour types

The type number after the flour shows its degree of nutrition. The number is in relation to the mineral weight that will remain after burning 100 g of that particular flour. For example, when burning type 405, the most commonly used flour, 405 mg minerals will remain. For type 1700, 1700 mg minerals can be measured on the scale. The higher the type number, the more nutritious the flour.

The different flour types are not available in the United States, so every kind of wheat flour can be used.

Liquid Glucose

Liquid glucose is a viscous, non-crystallising starch syrup. It is manufactured from potato and cornstarch. Cooking under pressure turns starch into glucose and dextrose. Liquid glucose prevents sugar from crystallising. For 500 g/18 oz sugar, a professional or ambitious amateur pastry chef uses 30 g liquid glucose. It cannot be purchased in regular retail stores. Ask your local baker who will surely sell you a small amount.

Unsweetened Cocoa Powder

Unsweetened cocoa powder is manufactured from roasted ground cocoa beans from which most of the oil and cocoa butter has been extracted. Cocoa powder with a low percentage of cocoa butter has a content of 10 percent to 20 percent, high percentage cocoa powders have a content of 20 percent to 24 percent.

Icings for Decorating

Coloured Icing

125 g/4 1/2 oz (1 cup)
  confectioners' sugar
2-3 tablespoons lemon juice
A few drops of food colouring,
  choose any colours you like

Sift confectioners' (icing) sugar and stir together with lemon juice until smooth. If desired, colour icing with food colouring. Since these colours are often very strong, it is better to mix the colour with 1 tablespoon of water first to ease adjustment. You can paint cookies however you like.

Cinnamon-Sugar Icing

125 g/4 1/2 oz (1 cup)
  confectioners' sugar
2 tablespoons cognac
5 g/1/4 oz ground cinnamon

For this quick icing, stir together sifted confectioners' sugar, ground cinnamon and cognac until smooth. Either apply icing onto cooled cookies with a brush or fill mixture into a small paper piping bag and garnish Christmas confectionery and other biscuits decoratively. This icing is especially suitable for Christmas cinnamon stars, since it intensifies their spicy taste.

Note:
All icing left-overs keep well when covered tightly with cling-film. When needed, add a few drops of water, alcohol or juice and stir until smooth. Pass through a fine mesh sieve and icing is soft again.

Egg White-Sugar Icing

Beat egg white with salt and one third of confectioners' sugar. As soon as egg whites begin to stiffen, gradually add remaining confectioners' sugar. Egg whites need to turn very stiff in between additions of confectioners' sugar. Last, stir in lemon juice. This egg white-sugar icing is especially suitable for decorating gingerbread houses, since the icing is flexible and dries rather quickly.

200 g/7 oz egg white

A pinch of salt

1 kg (2 1/4 lb) confectioners'
  sugar

1 tablespoon lemon juice

Spun Sugar Icing

Mix sugar with cold water and slowly bring to a boil. Skim off foam that rises to the surface just as water is about to boil with a tea sieve. Boil until temperature reaches 105 °C (220 °F), Gas mark 1/4.

125 g/4 1/2 oz (1 cup) sugar

90 ml/3 1/2 fl oz water

You can determine the right temperature even without a thermometer. Dip thumb and index finger first into ice water, then into the sugar syrup. If a thin thread forms between your fingers, the syrup has the right temperature. Brush hot icing onto warm biscuits with a brush. Move the brush back and forth a few times so icing turns white.

The Gloss of Chocolate Coating

As every amateur pastry chef knows – the temperature of the chocolate is crucial for the consistency of the coating and therefore for the glossy appearance of the baked goods.

If the temperature was too high, the chocolate does not dry well and turns grey and stiff. If the temperature was too low, the chocolate is too thick and is hard to apply.

How do you reach the right temperature for the chocolate and why does coating chocolate need to have a certain temperature? It is very simple: so the coating gets a beautiful matte gloss. Or, speaking in professional terms, only at a certain temperature does the cocoa butter combine with the remaining elements of the coating chocolate in such a way that a glossy, fast-drying and easy-to-use icing forms.

If you melt coating chocolate and leave it sitting out for some time, you can soon observe that the fatty parts separate and rise to the top. When you stir the chocolate they will disappear, yet fatty parts keep appearing until the right temperature is reached, thus ensuring a good bond.

This temperature is also called coating temperature by professionals. In practice: if you only have a regular pot at hand, stir liquid coating chocolate until the right coating temperature has been reached. This is best done if chocolate is placed into a heatproof bowl and set on top of a pan of water that is simmering. Chocolate starts to melt at 35 °C (75 °F). To turn out even more glossy coating chocolate, use the following trick: Brush part of the coating chocolate onto a cool marble plate. As soon as it hardens, scrape off chocolate, add to the remaining, liquid coating chocolate and melt again.

It is important that there is no draught. Liquid coating chocolate is very sensitive.

And one more thing: The higher the cocoa and cocoa butter content, the better and tastier chocolate. Very good quality chocolate has a cocoa portion of 71%, medium quality only 45%.

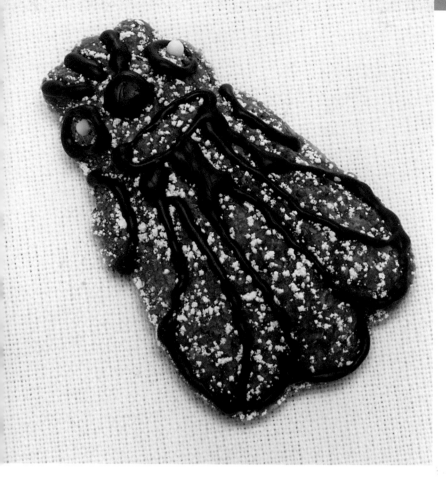

Liquid Chocolate
Icing

Yields for 100 cookies

125 g/4 oz dark coating chocolate

1 tablespoon liquid glucose (can be purchased in
   bakeries)

50 g/2 oz evaporated milk

In the end, the liquid icing is so viscous that it can be used for writing and decorating. The ideal temperature for this chocolate icing is 38 °C (80 °F). Icing always needs to have this temperature before it is filled into paper piping bag and used for decorating. Always cover icing well, otherwise it starts to harden at the top.

Note:
If you only have a little time, heat some hazelnut crème and use it for decorating your biscuits.

Finely chop coating chocolate, place into a heatproof bowl, set on top of a pan of simmering water and melt at 50 °C (110 °F). Stir liquid glucose into liquid chocolate using a spoon. Carefully add a dash of evaporated milk. While stirring constantly, melted chocolate turns thicker and starts to solidify. Add a few drops of evaporated milk again. The continued stirring separates the cocoa butter from the cocoa mass and the chocolate starts to crumble. Keep stirring, adding some more drops of evaporated milk, and eventually cocoa butter and cocoa mass will combine again. Now add the remaining evaporated milk while stirring constantly.

Fast & Easy Cookies

Hazelnut Spritz Cookies

Yields about 60 cookies

300 g/10 1/2 oz flour (type 405)

100 g/4 oz ground hazelnuts

1 teaspoon baking powder

250 g/9 oz unsalted butter

150 g/5 oz sugar

1 whole egg

A pinch of salt

Extract of 1/2 vanilla bean

A pinch of peel of organically grown lemon

75 ml/2 1/2 fl oz milk

❹ Add milk one tablespoon at a time and work in flour mixture with a plastic spatula. Fill dough into a piping bag or cookie press. Preheat oven to 190 °C (375 °F), Gas mark 5.

❺ Line cookie sheet with baking paper and pipe small circles onto cookie sheet. Bake in preheated oven for about 10 minutes.

❻ Cookies have an even more intense nut flavour if sprinkled with nuts before baking.

❶ All ingredients should be at room temperature.

❷ Sift flour and baking powder together, then combine with ground hazelnuts.

❸ Mix soft butter with sugar and a pinch of a salt. Add egg, then add scraped vanilla extract and lemon peel. Do not beat the mixture too foamy.

Spritz Cookies

200 g/7 oz soft unsalted butter

100 g/4 oz confectioners' sugar

1 teaspoon natural vanilla
    flavour

Peel of 1/2 organically grown
    lemon

1 egg

1 egg yolk

2 tablespoons rum

6-8 tablespoons milk

180 g/6 oz flour (type 405)

120 g/4 oz cornstarch

Oil and flour for baking sheet

Shortbread version:

❶ Cream together butter, confectioners' sugar and vanilla flavour. Gradually add lemon peel, egg and egg yolk and stir into a foamy mixture. Add rum and milk and quickly stir in mixture of flour and cornstarch. Do not stir for too long, otherwise dough will turn sticky. Refrigerate for at least 30 minutes.

❷ Preheat oven to 190 °C (375 °F), Gas mark 5. Grease cookie sheet with oil and dust with flour or line with baking paper.

❸ Fill mixture into piping bag with star tip No. 5 and pipe S-shaped loops, circles or mounds onto cookie sheet. Bake in hot oven on middle rack for about 10-15 minutes until golden brown.

125 g/4 oz soft unsalted butter

125 g/4 oz confectioners' sugar

1 tablespoon rum

1 egg

6-8 tablespoons milk

200 g/7 oz flour (type 405)

80 g/3 oz ground hazelnuts

Oil and flour for baking sheet

Coating chocolate for icing or
    confectioners' sugar for
    dusting

Crunchy version:

❶ The dough for the crunchy spritz cookies is prepared the same way as the shortbread version, but dough needs to be covered and refrigerated for at least 6 hours, best overnight.

❷ Pipe S-shapes or loops onto greased and floured cookie sheet and cool again for about 3-4 hours.

❸ Preheat oven to 200 °C (400 °F), Gas mark 6 and bake cookies for about 15-18 minutes until golden brown and crunchy.

Both types of cookies can be completely covered with coating chocolate at the right temperature or you can just dip the ends into liquid chocolate. You can also simply dust cookies with confectioners' sugar.

Each recipe yields about 45-50 cookies

Streusel Squares

❶ For the streusel preparation melt butter at 40 °C (85 °F). Combine sugar, finely ground almonds, flour and spices. Add liquid, not too hot butter and briefly knead all ingredients firmly together, or better rub between your fingers until small grains form. If necessary, loosely mix or rub streusel with your hands afterwards. This will help to connect them without getting too lumpy.

❷ For short bread dough, sift flour onto surface and make an indention in the flour mount using a tablespoon. Sift confectioners' sugar into indention with a sieve. Cut cold butter into small pieces and spread around the indention onto the flour. Place egg, almond milk and a pinch of salt into the middle and thoroughly chop all ingredients with a long knife. With cool hands rub the crumbs that have formed until they have a streusel-like consistency.

❸ Push dough into a ball or a rectangular and wrap in cling-film. It is best to refrigerate the dough overnight.

❹ The following day, preheat oven to 210 °C (415 °F), Gas mark 7. Knead dough briefly and roll to 3 mm (1/8 in) thickness on floured surface. Brush with egg yolk and evenly distribute streusel over dough. Bake in preheated oven for about 12 minutes until golden brown. Allow to cool lightly and cut into 4x4 cm (1 1/2 in) squares while still warm.

Note:
It is very important to prepare streusel with your hands. This way you can feel the right moment when the streusel are especially fluffy and not yet too compact. Only fluffy streusel will exhibit their particular short nature after baking. If you want to prepare them with a machine, use a dough kneading machine and press through a sieve with the appropriate mesh size afterwards. Streusel keep well for a few days in the refrigerator, but they can also be frozen without losing any quality.

Yields about 70 pieces

For streusel:
500 g/1 lb 2 oz unsalted butter
500 g/1 lb 2 oz sugar
50 g/2 oz finely ground almonds
900 g/2 lb flour (type 505)
A pinch of salt
Extract of 2 vanilla beans
Peel of 1 organically grown
   lemon
For shortbread dough:
300 g/10 1/2 oz flour (type 405)
200 g/7 oz unsalted butter
125 g/4 oz sugar
115 g/4 oz ground almonds
1 egg
1 tablespoon almond milk
A pinch of salt

Black-and-White Cookies

❶ For shortbread dough, cut butter into small pieces and knead together with confectioners' sugar, salt and vanilla extract, using your hands. Sift flour into mixture and quickly knead into a smooth dough. To make crunchy cookies, it is important that the butter does not get too warm while kneading.

❷ Halve dough and mix one half with sieved cocoa powder until dough has an even brown colouring. Wrap both parts in cling-film and refrigerate for 2 hours.

❸ Cut both doughs in half and shape into one dark and one light rope (3 cm/1 1/4 in Ø). Roll out the other halves in such a way that you can wrap dough sheet around each rope. Brush with egg yolk-cream mixture, to help glue doughs together better, and wrap dark dough sheet around light rope and light dough sheet around dark rope. Refrigerate for another hour.

❹ Preheat oven to 180 °C (350 °F) Gas mark 4. Cut into 1/2 cm (1/4 in) slices, place on cookie sheet lined with baking paper and bake for about 10-12 minutes.

Note:
Don't let cookies darken too much, otherwise they lose their black and white effect. Another alternative is to cut dough into thick strips, arrange in a chess pattern and wrap with dough sheet.

Yields about 75 cookies

300 g /10 1/2 oz butter
145 g/5 oz confectioners' sugar
Extract of 1/2 vanilla bean
A pinch of salt
400 g/14 oz flour (type 405)
35 g/1 1/2 oz unsweetened
    cocoa powder
1 egg yolk
2 tablespoons sweet cream

Raspberry Thumbprints

For the dough:

375 g/13 oz flour (type 405)

25 g/1 oz cornstarch

250 g/9 oz unsalted butter

150 g/5 oz confectioners' sugar

A pinch of salt

Peel of 1/2 organically grown
   lemon

Extract of 1/2 vanilla bean

For coating:

1 egg yolk

Sugar for sprinkling

8 tablespoons raspberry
   preserves

❶ Combine flour and cornstarch and sift together. Work in cold, diced butter, confectioners' sugar, salt, lemon peel and vanilla extract, and knead into a smooth dough. Add egg yolk.

❷ Now work in flour-cornstarch mixture, but don't knead dough. Just rub dough between your fingers so dough turns crumbly and has a similar consistency like streusel. Wrap in cling-film and refrigerate, preferably overnight.

❸ The following day, quickly knead on lightly floured surface. Separate into 2 parts and shape into ropes of 2.5 cm Ø each. Refrigerate again.

❹ Brush ropes with beaten egg yolk on all sides and roll in sugar. Refrigerate once more. Preheat oven to 180 °C (350 °F), Gas mark 4.

❺ Cut ropes into ca. 6 mm (1/4 in) slices. Make an indention in the middle of each slice with the handle of a wooden spoon.

❻ Pass raspberry preserves through a sieve and stir until smooth. Fill a dollop in the indention you made before. Bake in hot oven for about 10-12 minutes until golden brown.

Yields about 65 cookies

Chocolate Cookies

❶ Preheat oven to 160 °C (310 °F), Gas mark 3. Line cookie sheets with parchment paper. Baking paper is not suitable because cookies would expand too much sideways.

❷ Beat butter, confectioners' sugar, vanilla sugar and salt until foamy, but not too foamy. Gradually add egg yolks and stir in flour mixed with cocoa powder.

❸ Fill mixture into pastry bag with tip No. 7 and pipe small hemispherical mounds of 2 cm (3/4 in) Ø onto lined cookie sheet. Leave some distance between cookies since they will expand.

❹ Bake in hot oven for 10-15 minutes. Remove and allow to cool.

❺ Heat ginger preserves and brush onto cookie surface. Dry briefly, then dip in liquid coating chocolate and drip-dry on wire rack.

Yields about 40 cookies

200 g/7 oz unsalted butter
80 g/3 oz confectioners' sugar
20 g/3/4 oz vanilla sugar
A pinch of salt
4 egg yolks
20 g/3/4 oz unsweetened cocoa powder
200 g/7 oz flour (type 405)
For coating:
1/2 jar of ginger preserves
250 g/9 oz warm bitter-sweet coating chocolate

Egg Yolk Macaroons

250 g/9 oz marzipan

30 g/1 oz confectioners'
　　sugar

A pinch of salt

Peel of 1/4 organically grown
　　lemon

3 egg yolks

250 g/9 oz shortbread dough –
　　see page 24/25

Some sugar

Red currant jelly

1-2 tablespoons chopped
　　pistachios

❶ Crumble marzipan and place into mixing bowl. With a whisk, beat in confectioners' sugar, salt, lemon peel and gradually add egg yolk. Heat in top of a double boiler on slightly below boiling temperature to 70-80 °C (150 °F). Remove and stir until cooler.

❷ Preheat oven to 190 °C (375 °F), Gas mark 5. Prepare shortbread dough and cut cookies with spiky edge cookie cutter (5 cm/ 2 in Ø) . Place on cookie sheet lined with baking paper and bake for about 10 minutes.

❸ Fill macaroon mixture into piping bag with star tip No. 8 and pipe circles onto the cooled cookies. Reduce heat to 180 °C (350 °F), Gas mark 4 and bake for an additional 12 minutes.

❹ Fill middle of macaroons with red currant jelly and sprinkle with chopped pistachios.

Yields about 20-25 cookies

Cinnamon Waffles

100 g/4 oz flour

150 ml/5 fl oz sweet cream

2 egg yolks

1/2 teaspoon ground cinnamon

A pinch of ground cloves

Extract of 1 vanilla bean

40 g/1 1/2 oz liquid unsalted
butter

3 egg whites

A pinch of salt

30 g/1 oz sugar

Clarified butter for waffle iron

75 g/3 oz liquid unsalted butter

100 g/4 oz cinnamon sugar

❶ Sift flour into mixing bowl. Gradually stir in cream, egg yolks, spices, vanilla extract and butter. Beat egg white with a pinch of salt and half of the sugar until foamy. Once stiff peaks begin to form, add remaining sugar. Beat egg whites until stiff. First, fold one third of the stiff egg whites into the cream mixture, then fold in the rest.

❷ Preheat waffle iron and lightly grease with clarified butter. Place a dollop of dough into the centre, spread out and close the lid. Bake waffle at medium heat. Repeat procedure for all waffles and place on wire rack. Keep warm in oven at 120 °C (230 °F), Gas mark 1/4 or brush immediately with liquid butter and roll in cinnamon sugar.

Serves 6

Butter "S"

1 Cream butter and sieved confectioners' sugar together. Gradually add eggs and mix with lemon peel, salt and vanilla extract. Sift flour into mixture, knead into a ball and wrap in cling-film. Refrigerate for 8 hours.

2 Using a pastry bag, pipe 10 cm long dough pieces onto cookie sheet lined with baking paper and form them into "S"-shapes. Brush with beaten egg and sprinkle with coarse sugar. Preheat oven to 180 °C (350 °F), Gas mark 4.

3 Bake in preheated oven for about 12-15 minutes until golden brown.

Yields about 55-60 cookies

250 g/9 oz unsalted butter
  (at room temperature)
225 g/8 oz confectioners' sugar
2 eggs
1/4 teaspoon peel of organically
  grown lemon
Extract of 1/2 vanilla bean
A pinch of salt
500 g/1 lb 2 oz flour (type 405)
1 egg
80 g/3 oz coarse sugar

Cocoa-Nut "S"

1 Combine flour and cocoa powder and sift. Whisk butter, confectioners' sugar and spices together until creamy but not foamy. Preheat oven to 210 °C (420 °F), Gas mark 7.

2 Stir in eggs and bitter almond oil, then fold in flour and cocoa powder with a rubber spatula. Fill mixture into pastry bag with a small star tip and pipe dough into S-shapes onto cookie sheet lined with baking paper. Decorate with hazelnuts and bake for about 10 minutes in preheated oven until golden brown.

3 Allow cookies to cool after baking and decorate with very thin chocolate lines.

Yields about 70 cookies

375 g/13 oz flour (type 405)
50 g/2 oz unsweetened cocoa
  powder
250 g/9 oz unsalted butter
125 g/4 oz confectioners' sugar
1/2 teaspoon peel of organically
  grown lemon
A pinch of salt
2 eggs
5 drops bitter almond oil
90 g/3 1/2 oz unpeeled
  hazelnuts
Some warm liquid milk coating
  chocolate for decorating

Raisin Cookies

❶ Soak raisins in rum overnight.

❷ Sift flour together with baking soda. Knead marzipan with butter until smooth and mix with sugar. Add one egg at a time, then knead in flour-baking soda mixture. Quickly work in drained raisins.

❸ Preheat oven to 200 °C (400 °F), Gas mark 6. Thinly grease cookie sheet with liquid butter and lightly dust with flour. Fill dough into pastry bag with No. 11 tip and pipe rosette-shaped cookies of 3 cm (1 1/4 in) Ø onto cookie sheet. Leave enough room in between cookies since they will expand during baking.

❹ Bake cookies in preheated oven for about 15 minutes until golden brown. In the meantime, bring apricot preserves to a boil once. Brush finished cookies with preserves while hot and place in paper baking cups.

Note:
In addition, you can dredge cookies in vanilla sugar or decorate with chocolate lines.

Yields about 25 cookies

100 g/4 oz raisins

45 ml /2 fl oz rum

150 g flour (type 405)

1/2 teaspoon baking soda

25 g/1 oz marzipan

100 g /4 oz unsalted butter

100 g/4 oz sugar

2 eggs

100 g/4 oz apricot preserves

Honey-Nut Cookies

240 g/9 oz unsalted butter

120 g /1/3 cup honey

180 g/6 oz sugar

75 g/3 oz chopped hazelnuts

75 g /3 oz finely chopped candied
orange peel

2 teaspoons ground cinnamon

A pinch of powdered cloves

1/2 teaspoon potash

480 g /1 lb 1 oz flour (type 405)

❶ Bring butter, honey and sugar to a boil while stirring. Mix in hazelnuts, candied orange peel and spices. Prepare potash with a dash of lukewarm water and also stir into mixture. Sift flour onto work surface and make an indention in the middle. Pour warm butter-honey mixture into indention and knead until a smooth dough forms and all the flour is absorbed.

❷ Roll into two ropes (4-5 cm/2 in Ø), wrap in cling-film and refrigerate for 2 hours. Cut dough into 1/2 cm (1/4 in) slices with a knife. Preheat oven to 200 °C (400 °F, Gas mark 6).

❸ Line cookie sheet with baking paper and lay out cookies 5 cm (2 in) apart. Bake in preheated oven for about 10 minutes.

Yields about 60 cookies

Honey Coins

500 g/1 lb 2 oz honey-spice
dough – see page 23

125 g/4 oz sour cream

60 g/3 oz cookie crumbs

3 egg yolks

1/2 teaspoon ground cinnamon

A pinch of ground cloves

A pinch of bakers' ammonia

For coating:

500 g/1 lb 2 oz red currant
preserves

Dark coating chocolate

❶ Combine all ingredients into a smooth mixture. Fill in pastry bag with tip No. 9 and pipe hemispherical cookies (4 cm Ø) onto greased and floured cookie sheet.

❷ Make an indention in the middle of each cookie with a floured cooking spoon and bake at 200 °C (400 °F), Gas mark 6 for about 18 minutes.

❸ After baking, place a large dollop of red currant preserves into the indention and cover whole cookie with bitter chocolate coating. Place on wire rack and wait for chocolate coating to harden.

Yields about 12-15 cookies

Raspberry Breads

2 eggs

2 egg yolks

250 g/9 oz confectioners' sugar

A pinch of salt

225 g/8 oz flour (type 405)

35 g/1 1/2 oz cornstarch

320 g/10 1/2 oz raspberry
  preserves

❶ Beat whole eggs, egg yolks, confectioners' sugar and salt with a hand blender until thick and foamy. Pass 125 g (4 oz) raspberry preserves through a fine-mesh sieve and stir into foamy cream. Combine flour and cornstarch and sift into mixture. Fold in gently and evenly.

❷ Fill mixture into pastry bag with tip No. 5 and pipe hemispherical cookies (2 cm Ø) onto cookie sheet lined with baking paper. Make a small piping bag out of parchment paper, fill with a small amount of raspberry preserves and place a small red dot on about half the cookies. Allow to lightly dry in a warm dry place (if necessary in oven at 50 °C (110 °F)). Preheat oven to 190 °C (375 °F), Gas mark 5.

❸ Bake raspberry breads in oven for about 12 minutes. Cover flat side of cookies with the remaining raspberry preserves and stick always 2 cookies together in pairs.

Yields about 35 cookies

Butter Stars

5 egg yolks

75 g/3 oz confectioners' sugar

250 g/9 oz sour cream butter

350 g/12 oz flour (type 405)

A pinch of salt

A pinch of peel of organically
  grown lemon

100 g/4 oz vanilla sugar

❶ Place egg yolks into boiling water and let them set. Drain water and allow to cool. Pass egg yolks through a fine mesh sieve and knead into shortbread dough with remaining ingredients. Wrap in cling-film and refrigerate for about 2 hours. Preheat oven to 200 °C (400 °F), Gas mark 6.

❷ Roll dough to 8 mm (1/4 in) thickness, cut out stars and place on cookie sheet lined with baking paper. Bake in preheated oven for about 15 minutes until golden brown. Immediately dredge hot stars in vanilla sugar.

Yields about 45 cookies

Crunchy Sticks

❶ Coarsely cut butter into small pieces and knead with flour, confectioners' sugar, egg and orange peel into a smooth dough. Knead in crunchy muesli, wrap in cling-film and refrigerate for about 30 minutes.

❷ Preheat oven to 175°C (340 °F), Gas mark 4. Roll out dough on floured surface into a rectangular shape of 1 cm thickness. Cut rectangle into 8 cm long and 1-1.5 cm (1/2 in) thick sticks. Place sticks onto cookie sheet lined with baking paper and bake in preheated oven for about 15 minutes until golden brown. Remove from oven and allow to cool.

❸ In the meantime, coarsely chop coating chocolate, melt in top of a double boiler and cool to right temperature. Dip crunchy sticks halfway into the chocolate, give the sticks a gentle shake and place on baking paper. Sprinkle with pistachios and allow to dry.

Yields about 30-36 sticks

125 g/4 oz unsalted butter
250 g/9 oz flour (type 405)
80 g/3 oz confectioners' sugar
1 egg
Peel of 1 organically grown
   orange
100 g/4 oz crunchy muesli
150 g/5 oz milk coating
   chocolate
150 g/5 oz dark coating
   chocolate
20 g/3/4 oz chopped pistachios

Spice Squares

❶ Cream butter with confectioners' sugar, vanilla extract and lemon peel in a mixing bowl until foamy. Gradually add eggs and work in sifted flour, baking powder, grated chocolate and red wine using a wooden spoon. Preheat oven to 200 °C (400 °F), Gas mark 6.

❷ Grease round springform pan (28 cm Ø), fill with mixture and smooth out. Bake in preheated oven for about 20-25 minutes until golden brown. Remove from pan and allow to cool on wire rack.

❸ Stir together confectioners' sugar with rum until smooth. Brush onto cooled dough sheet and sprinkle with chopped hazelnut brittle. Cut into equal side triangles, 5 cm (2 in) long.

Yields about 25 cookies

125 g/4 oz unsalted butter
100 g/4 oz confectioners' sugar
Extract of 1/2 vanilla bean
1/2 teaspoon peel of organically
   grown lemon
2 eggs
125 g/4 oz flour (type 405)
1 teaspoon baking powder
70 g/3 oz grated chocolate
1/2 teaspoon honey-dough spice
   – see page 26
70 ml/3 fl oz red wine or hot
spice wine
<u>**For icing:**</u>
100 g/4 oz confectioners' sugar
3 tablespoons rum
60 g/2 oz hazelnut brittle

Chocolate Pretzels

125 g/4 oz unsalted butter
   (at room temperature)
50 g/2 oz confectioners' sugar
Extract of 1/2 vanilla bean
A pinch of salt
1 whole egg
1 egg yolk
210 g/7 oz flour (type 405)
10 g/1/2 oz cocoa powder
For icing:
Coloured icing – see page 34

❶ Beat butter, confectioners' sugar, vanilla extract and salt until foamy. Beat egg and egg yolk together and gradually add to mixture. Using a cooking spoon, add flour mixed with cocoa powder. Refrigerate dough for 1 hour. Roll dough to 5 mm (1/4 in) thickness in between cling-film and cut out pretzels. Place onto cookie sheet lines with baking paper and refrigerate for another 30 minutes.

❷ Preheat oven to 180 °C (350 °C), Gas mark 4. Bake pretzels for about 10 minutes and cool on wire rack.

❸ Decorate with coloured icing as desired and allow to dry.

Yields about 35 cookies

Chocolate Kisses

2 egg whites
150 g/5 oz sugar
125 g/4 oz roasted almond
   sticks
125 g/4 oz dark coating
   chocolate, grated
1 teaspoon amaretto

❶ Beat cold egg whites in a round mixing bowl with a hand blender. Gradually add sugar. As soon as egg whites are stiff, carefully fold in grated bitter chocolate, roasted almond sticks and amaretto with a spatula. Preheat oven to 160 °C (310 °F), Gas mark 3.

❷ Using 2 teaspoons, place small mounds of dough onto cookie sheet lined with baking paper. Dry cookies in preheated oven for about 10-12 minutes. Chocolate kisses still have to be soft in the middle since they will harden during the cooling process.

Yields about 45 cookies

Stollen & Gingerbread

Filling for Poppy Seed Stollen

500 g/1 lb 2 oz ground poppy
  seeds
1/2 l/2 cups milk
100 g/4 oz unsalted butter
270 g/9 1/2 oz coarse sugar
20 g/3/4 oz honey
200 g/7 oz cake crumbs
3 eggs
250 g/9 oz sultanas soaked
  in rum

❶ Quickly blanch poppy seeds in hot water and drain through very fine sieve. Bring milk, butter, sugar and honey to a boil. Remove from heat and add poppy seeds and cake crumbs. Allow poppy seed mixture to cool, then stir in eggs and sultanas.

❷ For a stollen of 1 kg you need 600 g/1lb 4 oz stollen dough without fruits and 400 g/14 oz poppy seed filling. There are 2 variations of poppy seed stollen. For the first variation, roll dough to 35 x 20 cm (14 x 8 in) and fill with poppy seed filling. Roll up from both sides and bake in a covered stollen mould.

❸ For the second variation, also roll out dough and cover with poppy seed mixture. Then roll up from one side only and place into stollen mould, seam side up. Close mould and allow dough to rise for 10 minutes before baking.

Filling for Butter-Nut-Stollen

325 g/11 1/2 oz finely ground
  hazelnuts
300 ml/10 fl oz milk
150 g/5 oz sugar
20 g/3/4 oz honey
200 g/7 oz cake crumbs
50 g/2 oz marzipan
50 g/2 oz apricot preserves
2 small eggs
A pinch of cinnamon
Extract of 1/2 vanilla bean

❶ Lightly roast ground hazelnuts in oven at 180 °C (350 °F), Gas mark 4 and allow to cool. Bring milk, sugar and honey to a boil. Remove from heat and add ground hazelnuts and cake crumbs. Knead marzipan, apricot preserves and eggs into a smooth dough. After nut mixture has cooled, work in marzipan dough.

❷ For a stollen of 1 kg you need 600 g/1lb 4 oz stollen dough without fruits and 400 g nut filling. You can prepare butter-nut stollen in 2 different ways, just like the poppy seed stollen (see above).

Note:
As a finish, stir 130 g/4 3/4 oz caramelised almonds into mixture.

Christmas Stollen

❶ Thoroughly mix all ingredients for the fruit mixture. Cover with foil and leave overnight in a warm place.

❷ For the pre-dough, firmly knead flour, yeast, cold milk and sugar for 15 minutes into a smooth dough with the kneading hook of mixer. Allow to rise in moderately warm place for about 30 minutes.

❸ For the main dough, beat all the ingredients with the exception of the marzipan, butter, spices and candied orange peel into a very soft dough. Then add pre-dough and process everything for an additional 10 minutes with kneading hook. Add finely chopped marzipan and knead until dough cleans the sides of the mixing bowl. Gradually add cold butter piece by piece until a homogeneous dough forms - the dough needs to display air bubbles. Finally, add spices and candied orange peel. Run dough on setting No. 1 and add soaked fruit mixture or even better, knead with your hands. Cover dough with kitchen towel and allow to rest for about 20 minutes.

❹ Carefully push dough together into a ball and allow to rest for an additional 10 minutes. Measure desired stollen weight and form dough into a longish round shape. Place into stollen mould, seam side up, and cover. Preheat oven to 190 °C (375 °F), Gas mark 5.

❺ Bake stollen in preheated oven for 5 minutes, then reduce temperature to 175 °C (345 °F), Gas mark 4. Bake for 50-60 minutes. After baking is finished, remove stollen from oven and immediately turn over onto a wire rack. Brush with hot butter and dredge in vanilla sugar.

For fruit mixture:
530 g/12 oz sultanas
65 g/2 1/2 oz candied citron peel
130 g/4 1/2 oz candied orange peel
130 g/1 cup almond sticks
2 cl rum
10 g/1/2 oz vanilla flavour
10 g/1/2 oz lemon flavour
50 ml/2 fl oz water

For pre-dough:
210 g/7 oz flour (type 550)
42 g/1 1/2 oz fresh yeast
150 ml/5 fl oz milk
1 tablespoon coarse sugar

For main dough:
220 g/8 oz flour (type 550)
A pinch of salt
4 g/1/4 oz stollen spice
100 ml/4 fl oz milk
1 small whole egg
2 egg yolks
25 g/1 oz sugar
20 g/3/4 oz quark (20% fat in solids)
150 g/5 oz marzipan
165 g/5 1/2 oz unsalted butter
10 g/1/2 oz lemon flavour
1 teaspoon vanilla flavour
25 g/1 oz candied orange peel, finely chopped
200 g/7 oz butter for mould
250 g/9 oz vanilla sugar

Marzipan Stollen

1 Sift flour into mixing bowl and make an indention in the middle. Crumble yeast into indention and dissolve with lukewarm milk. At the same time, mix in some flour from the edges. Dust pre-dough with flour and cover with kitchen towel. Allow to rise in a warm place for 30 minutes.

2 Knead egg, sugar, salt and spices together and add to pre-dough. Work into a smooth, firm dough, cover and allow to rise for 10 minutes.

3 In the meantime, knead butter and flour together until a soft dough forms. Knead in pre-dough and again allow to rise for 20 minutes. Mix sultanas, almonds, candied orange and citrus peel together. Quickly knead fruit mixture into yeast dough and allow to rise for 15 minutes one more time.

4 Roll dough to a rectangle. Thoroughly knead marzipan and Cointreau. Roll into a rope and place in the centre of the stollen dough. Fold the dough over and place stollen, seam side up, into the mould. Cover and preheat oven to 190 °C (375 °F), Gas mark 5.

5 Bake stollen in preheated oven for 5 minutes, then reduce temperature to 175 °C (345 °F), Gas mark 4. Bake for 50-60 minutes. After baking is finished, remove stollen from oven. Immediately turn over onto a wire rack, brush with hot butter and dredge in vanilla sugar.

500 g/1 lb 2 oz flour (type 405)
42 g/1 1/2 oz fresh yeast
200 ml/7 fl oz lukewarm milk
1 egg
40 g/1 1/2 oz sugar
A pinch of salt
Extract of 1/2 vanilla bean
1/2 teaspoon peel of organically
   grown lemon
220 g/8 oz unsalted butter
100 g/4 oz flour
150 g/5 oz sultanas soaked
   in rum
50 g/ 2 oz almond sticks
30 g/ 1 oz candied orange peel,
   chopped
60 g/2 1/2 oz candied citrus peel,
   chopped

250 g/9 oz marzipan
4 cl Cointreau

200 g/7 oz butter for greasing
250 g/9 oz vanilla sugar

Macadamia Nut Stollen

400 g/14 oz roasted macadamia
   nuts, coarsely chopped
150 g/5 oz honey
For the fruits:
50 g/2 oz candied citrus peel
70 g/3 oz candied orange peel
500 g/1 lb 2 oz sultanas
4 cl/1 fl oz rum
For the pre-dough:
420 g/15 oz flour (type 405)
55 g/2 oz fresh yeast
375 ml/13 fl oz milk
2 tablespoons sugar
For the main dough:
600 g/1 lb 5 oz flour (type 405)
3 eggs
200 ml milk
A pinch of salt
75 g/3 oz sugar
400 g/14 oz cold butter
10 g /1/2 oz stollen spice

1 For the macadamia nut stollen, soak macadamia nuts in honey for a week prior to baking. Heat honey to 40 °C (105 °F), then add nuts. Cover and place in a medium cold place.

2 Wash all ingredients for fruit mixture and mix thoroughly. Add rum, cover with cling-film and allow to rest in a warm place overnight.

3 For the pre-dough, knead milk, yeast, cold milk and sugar in mixer into a smooth dough. Refrigerate for 8 hours.

4 The following day, place macadamia nuts in a sieve, catching the honey in a dish.

5 For the main dough, work all ingredients with the exception of butter and spices into a very smooth dough. Then add pre-dough and knead everything in mixer for an additional 10 minutes. Gradually add butter, one piece at a time until a homogeneous dough forms – the dough needs to display air bubbles. Finally, add spices, fruit mixture and drained macadamia nuts and process on setting No. 1, or better knead everything with your hands. Cover with kitchen towel and allow to rise for 20 minutes.

6 Carefully press dough together into a ball and allow to rest for an additional 10 minutes. Measure desired weight and form into longish shape. Place in mould, seam side up, and cover. Preheat oven to 190 °C (375 °F), Gas mark 5.

7 Bake stollen in preheated oven for 5 minutes, then reduce temperature to 175 °C (345 °F), Gas mark 4. Bake for 50-60 minutes. After baking is finished, remove stollen from oven. Immediately turn over onto a wire rack and brush with honey from dish.

Fruit Bread

Very plain fruit bread recipes simply contain dried pears. More sophisticated versions are prepared with different nuts and other dried fruits.

1 Soak dried pears in water for 2-3 hours. Cook pears in the same water until soft and drain. Cut drained fruit into medium-size pieces.

2 Finely dice remaining dried fruits and mix with raisins and currants. Bring white wine and fruit schnapps to a boil and pour over fruit. Stir in walnuts and honey, cover and marinate overnight.

3 For the dough, knead all ingredients together, work in prepared fruit and allow to rise for 1 1/2 hours. Shape into 2 longish loaves.

4 Preheat oven to 180 °C (350 °F), Gas mark 4. Halve bread dough and roll into 2 rectangles big enough to wrap around fruit loaves.

5 Place fruit loaves onto bread dough sheets and wrap dough sheets around. Place onto greased cookie sheet, seam side down. Brush dough surface with milk and decorate with candied fruits, walnut halves and almonds as desired. Bake on lowest rack in preheated oven for about 45-60 minutes.

For fruit mixture:
125 g/4 1/2 oz dried pears
125 g/4 1/2 oz dried prunes
125 g/4 1/2 oz dried figs
125 g/4 1/2 oz dried apricots
125 g/4 1/2 oz dried dates
70 g/3 oz dried apples
25 g/1 oz candied citrus peel
25 g/1 oz candied orange peel
50 g/2 oz raisins
50 g/2 oz currants
200 ml/7 fl oz white wine
5 cl/2 fl oz fruit schnapps
100 g/4 oz walnuts, coarsely
  chopped
50 g/2 oz honey

For the dough:
100 g/4 oz wheat flour (type 550)
100 g/4 oz rye flour
10 g/1/2 oz yeast
100 ml/4 fl oz lukewarm water
8 g gingerbread spice –
  see page 26

500 g/1 lb 2 oz ready-made bread
  dough (can be purchased in
  bakeries)
Flour for cookie sheet
Milk for brushing
Candied fruits for decorating
Walnut halves and almonds for
decorating

Elisen Lebkuchen (Elisen Gingerbread)

❶ Mix ground nuts and almonds with 200 g/7 oz sugar. Stir marzipan and 3 egg whites together until smooth. Work marzipan mixture and nut-sugar mixture into a smooth dough.

❷ Beat remaining egg whites with a third of the remaining sugar until stiff and creamy. Gradually add the remaining sugar and keep beating until the egg whites have turned into firm, glossy peaks that can be cut.

❸ Stir one third of the egg whites into the nut mixture and carefully fold in the rest. Combine flour and spice mixture and fold into the dough with chopped candied orange and citrus peels. Dissolve bakers' ammonia in some water and add to dough.

❹ Fill dough into pastry bag with a large tip and pipe onto wafer rounds, leaving a thin edge. Leave Lebkuchen overnight. Decorate with almond halves before baking.

❺ The following day, preheat oven to 170 °C (352 °F) and bake Elisen Lebkuchen for about 20 minutes.

❻ Immediately brush with spun sugar icing after baking or cover Lebkuchen with coating chocolate of the right temperature after they have cooled.

Yields about 45 Lebkuchen

50 g/2 oz ground hazelnuts
50 g/2 oz ground peeled almonds
300 g/10 1/2 oz sugar
250 g/9 oz marzipan
6 egg whites
60 g/2 1/2 oz flour (type 405)
1 teaspoon Elisen Lebkuchen
    spice – see page 26
50 g/2 oz candied orange peel,
    finely chopped
50 g/2 oz candied citrus peel,
    finely chopped
1/2 teaspoon bakers' ammonia
50 g wafer rounds (Oblaten),
    5 cm/2 in Ø
Almonds, peeled and halved,
    for decorating

Nut Lebkuchen (Gingerbread)

① Crumble marzipan into a mixing bowl, add sugar and rub between your hands. Gradually add egg whites and stir smooth with a cooking spoon. Place mixture into a heatproof bowl and set on top of a pan of water that is lightly simmering. Add liquid glucose and beat with a whisk. The mixture should heat up to 45 °C (110 °F). If possible, verify with kitchen thermometer.

② Remove bowl and beat mixture with a hand blender until cold. Add bakers' ammonia dissolved in water.

③ Finely chop candied orange and citrus peel with chopping knife. Roast ground hazelnuts in dry pan and allow to cool. Mix everything with flour and stir evenly into foamy mixture with a cooking spoon.

④ Spread mixture about 1/2 cm (1/4 in) thick onto wafers, preferably using a broad knife. Calculate about 50 g/2 oz Lebkuchen mixture for each wafer. Place ready Lebkuchen next to each other onto cookie sheet. If desired, decorate with almonds and allow to dry well.

⑤ Preheat oven to 180 °C (350°F). Bake Lebkuchen in hot oven for about 15 minutes. Allow to cool and cover alternately with light and dark coating chocolate strips.

Note:
Decorate with cherries and halved almonds before baking. Finish hot Lebkuchen with spun sugar icing and allow to cool.

Yields about 18 Lebkuchen

150 g/5 oz marzipan
200 g/7 oz sugar
4 egg whites
20 g/3/4 oz liquid glucose
1/2 teaspoon bakers' ammonia
1 tablespoon water
30 g/1 oz candied orange peel
20 g/3/4 oz candied citrus peel
110 g/4 oz ground hazelnuts
70 g/3 oz flour (type 405)

Wafer rounds (Oblaten),
   7,5 cm/2 3/4 in Ø
Dark and light coating chocolate
   at coating temperature

Pointy Cake (Spitzkuchen)

625 g/1 lb 6 oz honey

475 g/1 lb 1 oz wheat flour
(type 550)

150 g/5 oz rye flour

5 g/1 teaspoon bakers' ammonia

1 g/1/4 teaspoon potash

Some egg white

250 g/9 oz sultanas

150 g/5 oz candied orange peel

4 cl/2 fl oz rum

100 g/4 oz chopped and roasted
almonds

10 g/1/2 oz gingerbread spice –
see page 26

300 g/10 1/2 oz dark coating
chocolate at coating temperature

1 Heat honey in a pot, afterwards allow to cool. Add different types of flour and knead into a smooth dough.

2 Dissolve bakers' ammonia with some water and potash in a little of the egg white. Work both ingredients thoroughly into dough, bakers' ammonia first, then potash.

3 Wash sultanas in hot water, dry and finely chop. Also finely chop candied orange peel, combine with raisins and marinate with rum for 1 hour. Knead with chopped almonds and gingerbread spice into the dough.

4 Preheat oven to 190 °C (375 °F), Gas mark 5. Roll dough into ropes as thick as your thumb and place on cookie sheet lined with baking paper. Bake in hot oven for about 20 minutes.

5 Cover baked dough ropes and allow to rest for about 2 days in a place with high humidity. With a knife, cut into trapezoid, bite-sized pieces.

6 Dip pointy cakes into dark coating chocolate at the right temperature. Dry on wire rack and drizzle with the remaining liquid coating chocolate after cooling.

Note:
Like all other honey or gingerbread cookies, pointy cake should be baked ahead of time, so when Christmas comes around they will have turned soft and are truly flavourful.

Yields about 90 pieces

White Lebkuchen

8 eggs

250 g/9 oz confectioners' sugar

100 g/4 oz honey

300 g/10 1/2 oz ground almonds

100 g/4 oz grated almonds

200 g/7 oz finely chopped candied orange peel

350 g/12 oz flour (type 405)

20 g/3/4 oz gingerbread spice – see page 26

1/2 teaspoon bakers' ammonia

A few drops of anise oil

Small wafer rounds (Oblaten)

200 g/7 oz confectioners' sugar for sprinkling

❶ Lightly beat eggs, confectioners' sugar and honey until foamy. Add ground and grated almonds as well as finely chopped candied orange peel. Work in sifted flour with a wooden spoon. Dissolve bakers' ammonia in a few drops of water and add to mixture. Finally stir in a few drops of anise oil.

❷ Spread onto wafer rounds and dry for about 12 hours. Preheat oven to 180 °C (350 °F), Gas mark 4 and bake for 20-25 minutes. Don't let them turn too dark. Sprinkle hot Lebkuchen generously with confectioners' sugar and allow to cool.

Yields about 45 Lebkuchen

Coconut Lebkuchen

❶ Mix all ingredients together with the exception of the flour and allow to rise for about 1 hour. Place in top of a double boiler and heat until dough cleans sides of the pot, while stirring constantly. Spread mixture onto wafer rounds as thick as a finger while still warm.

❷ Dry Lebkuchen for 8 hours. Preheat oven to 190 °C (375 °F), Gas mark 5 and bake for about 18 minutes. Cool and cover with coating chocolate.

Yields about 30 Lebkuchen

6 egg whites

370 g/13 oz sugar

250 g/9 oz coconut flakes

25 g/1 oz candied citrus peel

25 g/1 oz candied orange peel

1 tablespoon honey

A pinch of lemon peel

Wafer rounds (Oblaten),
    9 cm/3 1/2 in Ø

30 g/1 oz flour (type 405)

White coating chocolate at
    coating temperature

International Classics

Germany

Butter Speculatius Biscuits

200 g/7 oz unsalted butter

**300 g/10 1/2 oz confectioners'
sugar**

100 ml/4 fl oz milk

1/4 teaspoon bakers' ammonia

500 g/1 lb 2 oz flour (type 405)

**5 g/1/4 oz speculatius spice –
see page 26**

A pinch of salt

**Peel of 1/2 organically grown
lemon**

Flour for dusting of moulds

Milk and sugar for brushing

❶ Knead very cold butter together with confectioner's sugar. Dissolve bakers'
ammonia in milk, then add to butter mixture with remaining ingredients.
Crumble dough between your fingers (similar to the preparation of streusel).
Loosely distribute over cookie sheet and refrigerate overnight.

❷ The following day, briefly knead dough streusel and roll out to 3 mm/ 1/8 in
thickness. Cut into rectangles the size of the speculatius moulds (springerle
moulds).

❸ Dust moulds with flour and place dough sheet over them. With a rolling pin
roll over dough, pressing it into the mould. Cut off overlapping dough with a
thin wire or a sharp knife.

❹ Knock onto moulds to release biscuits and place on cookie sheet lined with
baking paper and sprinkled with grated almonds. Brush with lightly sugared
milk. Preheat oven to 200 °C (400 °F), Gas mark 6.

❺ Bake speculatius biscuits in preheated oven for 15-20 minutes until golden
brown. Allow to cool and store biscuits in tin jars.

Yields about 55-60 biscuits

Spice Speculatius Biscuits

❶ Knead very cold butter together with brown sugar. Work in cookie crumbs and milk, then add egg yolk and remaining ingredients. Crumble dough between your fingers (similar to the preparation of streusel). Loosely distribute over cookie sheet and refrigerate overnight.

❷ The following day, briefly knead dough and roll out to 3 mm/ 1/8 in thickness using a rolling pin. Cut into rectangles about the size of the speculatius moulds (springerle moulds).

❸ Dust moulds with flour and place dough sheet over them. With a rolling pin roll over dough, pressing it into the mould. Cut overlapping dough with a thin wire or a sharp knife.

❹ Knock onto moulds to release biscuits and place on cookie sheet lined with baking paper. Brush with milk. Repeat procedure until all the dough is used up. Preheat oven to 180 °C (350 °F) Gas mark 4.

❺ Bake speculatius biscuits in preheated oven for 15-20 minutes until golden brown. Allow to cool and store biscuits in tin jars.

Yields about 55-60 biscuits

275 g/9 1/2 oz unsalted butter
325 g/11 oz fine brown sugar
100 g/4 oz cookie crumbs
50 ml/2 fl oz milk
1 egg yolk
75 g/3 oz finely ground almonds
550 g/1 lb 4 oz flour (type 405)
A pinch of salt
Flour for dusting of moulds
Milk for brushing

Stuffed Marzipan Balls

For biscuit batter:

3 egg yolks

65 g/2 1/2 oz sugar

4 egg whites

55 g/2 oz cornstarch

30 g/1 oz flour (type 405)

For the stuffing:

120 g/4 oz unsalted butter

75 g/3 oz dark coating chocolate

2 cl/1 fl oz rum

3 egg whites

100 g/4 oz confectioners' sugar

100 g/4 oz raspberry jelly

500 g/1 lb 2 oz marzipan

300 g/10 1/2 oz confectioners' sugar

100 g/4 oz unsweetened cocoa powder

❶ Lightly cream egg yolks and half of the sugar. Beat egg whites until stiff peaks begin to form, gradually add remaining sugar and continue beating until egg white is very stiff and glossy.

❷ First add sifted cornstarch to egg whites, then beaten egg yolks, and last fold in sifted flour.

❸ Preheat oven to 190 °C (375 °F), Gas mark 5. Fill batter into pastry bag with tip No. 10 and pipe hemispherical mounds (3cm/ 1 1/4 in Ø) onto cookie sheet lined with baking paper. Bake in preheated oven for 8-10 minutes until golden brown.

❹ For chocolate cream, beat butter until foamy and stir in melted coating chocolate and rum. Beat egg whites until very stiff, gradually adding sugar. Carefully fold into butter mixture.

❺ Hollow out baked biscuit balls from the inside. Fill with chocolate cream and glue 2 halves together. Briefly bring raspberry jelly to a boil and brush onto balls on all sides.

❻ Knead marzipan and 200 g/ 7 oz confectioners' sugar together into a smooth dough. Dust working surface with remaining confectioners' sugar and roll marzipan dough to 2 mm/ 1/8 in thickness. Cut into squares, wrap around biscuit balls and dredge in cocoa powder.

Yields about 25 balls

Anise Cookies

3 eggs

1 egg yolk

300 g/10 1/2 oz sugar

A pinch of salt

2 drops vanilla flavour

Peel of 1/2 organically grown
   lemon

12 drops anise oil

300 g/10 1/2 oz flour (type 405)

Liquid butter for cookie sheet

Flour for dusting

1 tablespoon anise for sprinkling

❶ Place whole eggs, egg yolks, sugar and salt into a heatproof bowl, set on top of a pan of simmering water and whisk together (ideal temperature: 43 - 50 °C (100 °F)). Place in food processor and process on highest setting for 10 minutes. Reduce speed to medium and process for an additional 5 minutes. Add vanilla flavour, lemon peel and anise oil. Gradually work in sifted flour one tablespoon at a time. Fill batter into pastry bag with No. 5 tip.

❷ Lightly grease cookie sheet with butter, dust with flour and sprinkle with anise. Pipe even mounds onto sheet and allow to dry in a low humidity place for about 30 minutes. Do not dry for too long, other wise cookies will turn hollow during baking. Preheat oven to 170 °C (325 °F), Gas mark 3.

❸ Place cookies in preheated oven and bake for 15 minutes, keeping the oven door ajar. Anise cookies keep well in airtight containers.

Yields about 65-70 cookies

Nut-Clove Sticks

140 g/5 oz ground almonds

120 g/4 oz ground hazelnuts

250 g/9 oz sugar

Extract of 1/2 vanilla bean

A pinch of ground cloves

2 eggs

For the icing:

1 egg white

120 g/4 oz confectioners' sugar

A pinch of ground cloves

❶ Combine almonds, hazelnuts and sugar in a mixing bowl. Add vanilla extract, ground cloves and eggs, and knead into a dough. Wrap in cling-film and refrigerate for 1 hour. Roll dough to 1/2 cm/ 1/4 in thickness on floured surface, cut into 2 x 5 cm/ 3/4 x 2 in long sticks and place on cookie sheet lined with baking paper.

❷ Beat egg whites until stiff, gradually sifting in confectioners' sugar. Add ground cloves and spread mixture onto nut sticks. Preheat oven to 200 °C (400 °F), Gas mark 6.

❸ Bake cookies in preheated oven for about 12 minutes.

Yields about 65-70 cookies

Cinnamon Stars

1 Lightly roast almonds and hazelnuts in oven at 180 °C (350 °F), Gas mark 4 and allow to cool. Stir marzipan, sugar and egg white into a smooth creme, then add ground cinnamon, spices, salt and lemon peel. Afterwards work in roasted hazelnuts and almonds and candied orange peel. Place cinnamon cream into a mixing bowl, sprinkle with 1 tablespoon of the nuts and refrigerate overnight.

2 The following day, briefly whisk egg whites with hand blender until light and foamy. Add one fifth of the confectioners' sugar first. As soon as egg whites rise in volume, gradually drizzle in remaining confectioners' sugar. Continue beating until egg whites turn firm and stiff. Now add lemon juice. This adds additional stability to the whisked egg whites.

3 Briefly knead nut mixture. In case dough is too soft, add additional ground nuts. Sprinkle cookie sheet with remaining ground nuts and roll out mixture to 1 cm/ 1/2 in thickness. Briefly place in freezer.

4 Brush cooled dough sheet with egg white icing and cut out stars. Keep dipping cookie cutter into water. Preheat oven to 150 °C (300 °F), Gas mark 2.

5 Slowly bake cinnamon stars in preheated oven. Stars should only darken at the bottom.

Yields 75-80 cookies

160 g/5 1/2 oz ground almonds
160 g/5 1/2 oz ground hazelnuts
160 g/5 1/2 oz marzipan
500 g/1 lb 2 oz sugar
6 egg whites
1 tablespoon ground cinnamon
1 teaspoon ground cloves
A pinch of salt
Peel of 1 organically grown
   lemon
60 g/2 1/2 oz candied orange
   peel, finely chopped
About 50 g/2 oz grated hazelnuts
For Icing:
2 egg whites
320 g/11 oz confectioners' sugar
1 tablespoon lemon juice

Bethmännchen ("Praying Men")

❶ Mix all ingredients into a smooth mixture. Roll marzipan mixture into a rope and cut into 10 g/ 1/2 oz pieces. Form pieces into small balls with your hands and with some egg white glue 3 almonds on each side.

❷ Leave prepared Bethmännchen sitting out overnight. The following day, bake in oven under high heat from above until golden brown. After they have cooled down, dip bottom into liquid coating chocolate so Bethmännchen get dark "feet" and don't dry out from below.

Yields about 60 pieces

500 g/1 lb 2 oz marzipan
50 g/2 oz confectioners' sugar
50 g/2 oz honey
Peel of 1/2 organically grown
  lemon
5 drops of rose water
1 beaten egg white
180 peeled and halved almonds
Dark coating chocolate at
  coating temperature

Snow Cubes

❶ Knead sifted flour, butter, egg yolks, sugar and rum into a shortbread dough, wrap in cling-film and refrigerate for 1 hour. Roll dough to 3 mm/ 1/8 in thickness, place on cookie sheet lined with baking paper and bake at 180 °C (350 °F), Gas mark 4 for about 12-15 minutes until golden brown. Allow to cool, spread with smoothed out apricot preserves and sprinkle with cookie crumbs.

❷ Beat very cold egg whites until foamy, using a hand mixer. Gradually add sugar and keep beating until snow is stiff and glossy. Spread mixture onto dough sheet and sprinkle with almond sticks. Place in oven at 140 °C (350 °F), Gas mark 4 and bake for another 15 minutes, but don't let cookies get dark. Cut into 2 x 2 cm/ 3/4 in cubes.

Yields about 25 cookies

250 g/9 oz flour (type 405)
125 g/4 1/2 oz cold unsalted
  butter
4 egg yolks
30 g/1 oz sugar
2 tablespoons rum
100 g/4 oz apricot preserves
2 tablespoons cookie crumbs
4 egg whites
125 g/4 1/2 oz sugar
50 g/2 oz almond sticks

Vanilla Pretzels

40 g/1 1/2 oz marzipan

5 egg yolks

750 g/1 lb 10 oz flour (type 405)

250 g/9 oz confectioners' sugar

500 g/1 lb 2 oz cold unsalted
    butter

A pinch of salt

Peel of 1 organically grown
    lemon

Extract of 1 vanilla bean

Flour for rolling out dough

For icing:

200 g/7 oz confectioners' sugar

10 g/1/2 oz vanilla flavour

2 tablespoons lemon juice

5 cl/2 fl oz Cointreau

❶ Stir marzipan together with egg yolks until smooth.

❷ Sift flour onto surface and with a tablespoon make an indention in the middle. Add sifted confectioners' sugar into indention. Cut butter into small pieces and spread around the indention onto the flour. Place egg yolk-marzipan mixture into the indention and thoroughly chop all ingredients with a long knife.

❸ With cold hands rub the crumbs that have formed until they have a streusel-like consistency. Push dough streusel together into a rectangle and wrap in cling-film. Refrigerate, preferably overnight.

❹ Push dough into a ball or a rectangular and wrap in cling-film. It is best to refrigerate the dough overnight.

❺ The following day briefly knead dough and roll to 3 mm/ 1/8 in thickness on floured surface. Cut out pretzels, dipping cookie cutter in flour from time to time. Preheat oven to 200 °C (400 °F), Gas mark 6.

❻ Bake in preheated oven until golden brown. For the icing, mix all ingredients together until smooth. Dredge warm pretzels through the icing with a fork and dry on wire rack.

Note:

You can also coat vanilla pretzels with coloured icing and decorate them with sugar pearls and other colourful sweets if desired. Attached to red bows, they make great Christmas tree ornaments. Don't let the large dough amount scare you. You will soon see how these delicious pretzels vanish before your eyes.

Yields about 110 pretzels

Aachener Printen (Aachen Bars)

❶ Combine honey, sugar, water and salt in a mixing bowl, place into a heatproof bowl, set on top of a pan of simmering water and stir until all sugar crystals have dissolved. Set bowl into another bowl filled with ice cubes and stir mixture until cold. Gradually add different types of flour.

❷ Whisk potash with whole eggs and egg yolk and dissolve bakers' ammonia in lukewarm milk. Mix spices, lemon peel, nuts, candied orange peel and candy sugar together. First knead potash into dough, then add remaining ingredients with dissolved bakers' ammonia and knead into basic dough. Refrigerate for 1 hour.

❸ Preheat oven to 200 °C (400 °F), Gas mark 6. Roll dough out on floured surface to 4 mm thickness and cut into 3 x 6 cm/ 1 1/4 x 2 1/2 in rectangles. Place onto cookie sheet lined with baking paper and brush with milk. Bake in preheated oven for 15-20 minutes until crisp. Remove ready printen from cookie sheet and store in refrigerator. Brush with water once a day for 5 consecutive days to turn them soft.

250 g/9 oz honey
75 g/3 oz sugar
1 tablespoon water
A pinch of salt
170 g/6 oz wheat flour (type 550)
170 g/6 oz rye flour
2 tablespoons potash
2 whole eggs
1 egg yolk
2 tablespoons bakers' ammonia
50 ml/2 fl oz milk
A pinch of ground cinnamon
A pinch of ground cardamom
1/2 teaspoon gingerbread spice – see page 26
Extract of 1/2 vanilla bean
1/2 teaspoon peel of organically grown lemon
100 g/4 oz finely ground hazelnuts
100 g/4 oz candied orange peel, chopped
500 g/1 lb 2 oz candy sugar

Almond Printen (Almond Bars)

❶ Heat honey, sugar and butter while stirring, until sugar has dissolved. Allow to cool lightly, then work in sifted flour, chopped almonds, spices and potash dissolved in water. Place into mixing bowl, cover and refrigerate for 1 hour.

❷ Preheat oven to 190 °C (375 °F), Gas mark 5. Dust dough thoroughly with flour and roll to about 1 cm/ 1/2 in thickness. Sprinkle with almond leaves and lightly press into dough with rolling pin. Cut into 3 x 4 cm/ 1 1/4 x 1 1/2 in rectangles and place onto cookie sheet lined with baking paper. Bake in preheated oven for 18 minutes.

250 g/9 oz honey
80 g/3 oz unsalted butter
80 g/3 oz brown sugar
1 teaspoon potash
380 g/13 oz flour (type 405)
50 g/2 oz peeled almonds, finely chopped
1 teaspoon gingerbread spice – see page 26
80 g/3 oz almond leaves for sprinkling

Yields about 30-35 printen each

Coconut Macaroons

1 Thoroughly mix flaked coconut, sugar, salt and egg whites. Place into a pot and roast over low heat, stirring continuously with a wooden spoon. Once mixture has reached a temperature of 55 - 60 °C (110 °F) and easily leaves the bottom of the pot, remove from heat. Fill into mixing bowl and stir in fruits and lemon peel.

2 Cool batter to room temperature and pipe onto prepared wafer rounds using piping bag with tip No. 10. Preheat oven to 200 °C (400 °F), Gas mark 6.

3 Bake lightly dried coconut macaroons in oven for about 15 minutes. Leave oven door ajar.

Yields about 60 macaroons

250 g/9 oz flaked coconut

375 g/13 oz sugar

A pinch of salt

6 egg whites

30 g/1 oz candied orange peel,
    finely chopped

20 g/3/4 oz candied citrus peel,
    finely chopped

Peel of 1/2 organically grown
    lemon

Wafer rounds (Oblaten)
    6 cm/2 1/2 in Ø

Almond Meringue

1 Beat egg white with 100 g/ 4 oz sugar until stiff peaks form and egg white is firm enough to be cut. Combine remaining sugar, lemon peel and almonds and fold into whisked egg whites. Spread mixture onto wafer rounds in a dome shape using a knife and place onto cookie sheet.

2 Preheat oven to 150 °C (300 °F), Gas mark 2. Bake almond meringue on middle rack for about 25 minutes. Do not allow meringue to darken or get too dry.

3 Stir sifted confectioners' sugar with water and vanilla sugar until smooth. Brush warm meringue with icing and allow to cool.

Yields about 25 cookies

2 egg whites

150 g/5 oz sugar

100 g/4 oz peeled almonds, finely
    ground

1/4 teaspoon peel of organically
    grown lemon

Wafer rounds (Oblaten)
    6 cm/2 1/2 in Ø

For icing:

150 g/5 oz confectioners' sugar

1 teaspoon vanilla sugar

2 tablespoons warm water

Chocolate-Coconut Macaroons

300 g/10 1/2 oz flaked coconut

350 g/12 oz sugar

6 egg whites

20 g/1 oz cocoa powder

100 g/4 oz candied orange peel,
    finely chopped

1 tablespoon lemon juice

A pinch of ground cinnamon

150 g/5 oz light coating
chocolate at the right coating
    temperature

❶ Thoroughly mix flaked coconut, sugar, egg whites, salt and cocoa powder in a pot. Carefully roast over medium heat while stirring with a wooden spoon. Once mixture has reached a temperature of 55-60 °C (110 °F), and easily leaves the bottom of the pot, remove from heat and fill into a mixing bowl. Mix in candied orange peel and lemon juice.

❷ Allow mixture to cool to room temperature. Fill into pastry bag with tip No. 10 and pipe little mounds onto cookie sheet lined with baking paper. Preheat oven to 200 °C (400 °F), Gas mark 6.

❸ Lightly dry coconut macaroons, then bake in preheated oven for about 15 minutes. Leave oven door ajar. After macaroons have cooled down, dip halfway into coating chocolate.

Yields about 40 macaroons

Date Rolls

170 g/6 oz dried dates

125 g/4 1/2 oz peeled almonds

30 g/1 oz tender oats

40 g/1 1/2 oz crème fraîche

1/2 teaspoon ground cinnamon

2 tablespoons rose water

1/2 teaspoon peel of organically
    grown lemon

1 teaspoon lemon juice

Sugar for surface

100 g/4 oz fine brown sugar

❶ Pit dates and chop finely. Chop one half of the almonds coarsely, the other half finely. Combine with remaining ingredients in a mixing bowl.

❷ Sprinkle surface with sugar. Take one teaspoon of batter each time and shape into 5 - 8 cm/ 2 - 3 in long rolls. Preheat oven to 180 °C (350 °F), Gas mark 4. Place on cookie sheet lined with baking paper and bake in preheated oven for about 12-15 minutes. Still warm, roll in brown sugar. Wrap in silver foil.

Yield about 40-45 rolls

Gingerbread Bear Paws

225 g/8 oz finely ground hazelnuts

3 eggs

250 g/9 oz sugar

175 g/6 oz marzipan

150 g/5 oz flour (type 405)

60 g/2 1/2 oz unsweetened cocoa powder

25 g/1 oz candied citrus peel, chopped very finely

25 g/1 oz candied orange peel, chopped very finely

Coating chocolate at the right coating temperature

1 Lightly roast hazelnuts in oven at 180 °C (350 °F), Gas mark 4 and allow to cool. Cream eggs and sugar together. Knead marzipan together with hazelnuts. Add egg mixture and flour sifted together with cocoa powder. Finally add candied citrus and orange peel.

2 Preheat oven to 190 °C (375 °F), Gas mark 5. Shape dough into rolls and cut into pieces. Form small balls, roll in sugar and press into buttered paw moulds. Bake in preheated oven for about 15 minutes. Decorate with coating chocolate as desired.

Yields about 30 cookies

Pfeffernüsse

1 Cream eggs, sugar and salt with a hand blender. Gradually fold in flour, candied orange and citrus peels with a spatula. Then work in bakers' ammonia dissolved in water and refrigerate dough overnight.

2 Preheat oven to 200 °C (400 °F), Gas mark 6. Roll dough to 1 cm/ 1/2 in thickness on floured surface and cut out small cookies the size of hazelnuts. Place onto cookie sheet lined with baking paper and bake in preheated oven for about 13 minutes.

Yields about 140 cookies

4 eggs

500 g/1 lb 2 oz sugar

A pinch of salt

600 g/1 lb 5 oz flour (type 405)

125 g/4 1/2 oz candied orange peel, finely chopped

20 g/1 oz gingerbread spice – see page 26

Peel of 1/2 organically grown lemon

1 teaspoon bakers' ammonia

Hazelnut Crescents

140 g/5 oz ground hazelnuts

400 g/14 oz unsalted butter

140 g/5 oz confectioners' sugar

A pinch of salt

1/4 teaspoon peel of organically
   grown lemon

Extract of 3 vanilla beans

560 g/1 lb 4 oz flour (type 405)

Vanilla sugar mixed with
   confectioners' sugar for
   dredging

❶ Roast hazelnuts in a skillet without any oil until golden brown, spread out and allow to cool.

❷ Quickly stir together butter, confectioners' sugar, salt, lemon peel and vanilla extract. Do not cream butter, otherwise crescents lose their shape during baking.

❸ Combine flour and cooled hazelnuts and work one third into butter mixture. Rub dough between your fingers to form crumbs. Dough needs to have a streusel-like consistency. Wrap in cling-film and refrigerate for 1 - 2 hours.

❹ Knead in remaining flour-nut mixture quickly with cold hands until a smooth, workable dough forms. Make sure not to knead dough for too long, otherwise dough will turn brittle.

❺ Preheat oven to 200 °C (400 °F), Gas mark 6. Cut out small portions of about 15-20 g/ 3/4 oz from dough and form into small rolls with thin tips (crescent shapes).

❻ Lay out on cookie sheet lined with baking paper and bake in preheated oven for about 14 minutes. Carefully remove crescents from cookie sheet and immediately roll in vanilla-confectioners' sugar.

Yields about 75 cookies

Vanilla Crescents

❶ Sift flour and baking powder onto work surface.

❷ Dice butter and knead together with confectioners' sugar. Add vanilla extract and salt. Gradually knead egg whites into dough, then add roasted almonds.

❸ Rub dough and flour between your fingers until mixture has a streusel-like consistency. Place dough into a mixing bowl, cover with cling-film and refrigerate overnight.

❹ The following day, knead dough once more and separate into 5 pieces. From the individual parts shape 1/2 cm/ 1/4 in thick ropes. Cut into 2 cm/ 3/4 in long pieces and shape into crescents. Just roll dough on a cutting board or table. You can also shape small rolls with your fingers and pinch tips. Place crescents onto a cookie sheet lined with baking paper and bend into a half-moon shape. Cool cookie sheet before baking. Preheat oven to 175 °C (330 °F), Gas mark 3 1/2.

❺ Bake vanilla crescents in preheated oven for about 15 minutes not too dark. Immediately after baking, dredge crescents in vanilla sugar.

Yields about 65 cookies

500 g/1 lb 2 oz flour (type 405)
3 g/1/4 oz baking powder
350 g/12 oz cold unsalted butter
175 g/6 oz confectioners' sugar
Extract of 2 vanilla beans
A pinch of salt
2 1/2 egg whites
100 g/4 oz grated roasted almonds
Vanilla sugar for dredging

Baumkuchen (Layered Cake)

50 g/2 oz marzipan

2 cl cherry schnapps

7 egg yolks

120 g/4 1/2 oz soft unsalted
butter

1 tablespoon liquid glucose

Peel of 1 organically grown
lemon

Extract of 1 vanilla bean

8 egg whites

A pinch of salt

125 g/ 4 1/2 oz sugar

65 g/2 1/2 oz cornstarch

65 g/2 1/2 oz flour (type 405)

A pinch of baking powder

8 cl/3 fl oz orange liquor for
soaking

200 g/7 oz dark coating
chocolate and coloured icing

3 tablespoons raspberry jelly

It is important for this recipe that all ingredients have the same temperature. It is best to measure out the ingredients on the previous day and have them ready for the next day.

1 Turn on heat from above in oven and line cookie sheet with baking paper.

2 Whip together marzipan, cherry schnapps and 2 egg yolks until smooth. Cream glucose syrup, butter and flavours together, gradually add remaining egg yolks. Combine with marzipan dough.

3 Beat egg whites with salt, sugar and cornstarch until creamy and very stiff. First stir in one third of the whisked egg whites into the dough, then carefully fold in the rest. Last, fold in sifted flour mixed with baking powder.

4 Distribute a few tablespoons of batter evenly into a rectangular springform pan using a spatula. Bake in preheated oven (200 °C (350 °F), Gas mark 4) on middle rack until golden brown.

5 Spread another thin layer of dough on top and bake on the uppermost rack. Keep repeating procedure, baking all but the last layer on upper rack until all the batter is done. The last layer should be baked on the middle rack again. Allow cake to cool inside the cake form so it loses steam slowly and stays especially juicy.

6 After cake has cooled, turn over onto work surface and cut into rhombus shapes. Soak with orange liqueur, wrap in cling-film and refrigerate overnight. The next day, cover with coating chocolate that has the right temperature and garnish as desired with sugar icing and raspberry jelly.

Yields about 85 pieces

Dominosteine
(Domino Stones)

500 g/1 lb 2 oz honey-spice
   dough – see page 23

For jelly-filling:

20 g/1 oz agar-agar

1/2 l/17 fl oz (2 cups) red wine

175 g/6 oz sugar

500 g/1 lb 2 oz red current
   preserves

100 g/4 oz marzipan

For coating:

500 g/1 lb 2 oz dark coating
   chocolate at coating
   temperature

1 Roll honey-spice dough into a rectangular sheet with a thickness of 6 mm/ 1/4 in. Place on cookie sheet lined with baking paper and bake at 175 °C (330 °F), Gas mark 3 1/2 for about 15 minutes.

2 Cut honey-spice dough sheet in half lengthwise so you get two 3 mm/ 1/8 in thick sheets. Cover one of the plates on one side with dark coating chocolate. Once coating chocolate has hardened, place onto cookie sheet, chocolate side down and frame dough sheet.

3 Soak agar-agar in cold water for 24 hours. In a pot, bring soaked agar-agar and wine to a boil, add sugar and red currant jelly and bring to a rolling boil once more. The firmness of the jelly depends upon the cooking time, therefore keep testing jelly consistency during cooking. Allow mixture to cool.

4 Roll marzipan to 3 mm/ 1/8 in thickness and cut to the same size as the frame. Use left-over marzipan to cover up any holes between honey-spice dough and frame. Shortly before jelly hardens, pour into the prepared frame and allow to cool. Place marzipan sheet on top of jelly.

5 Allow to rest in a cool place for 1 day. Thinly cover the surface with coating chocolate. Cut layers into cubes, 2.5 x 2.5 cm/ 1 x 1 in, and thinly cover with coating chocolate that has the right temperature. It is recommended to attach a thin wire on top of the mixing bowl with the coating chocolate, so you can clean the fork on the wire as you take out dominosteine. Only 3/4 of the dominosteine should sit on the fork. To set dominosteine down, tilt fork in the back so you can set dominstein onto baking sheet at an angle.

Yields about 50 pieces

Liegnitzer Bomben (Liegnitz Pastries)

The original recipe produces a sweet that is 10 cm/ 4 in high and has a diameter of 8 - 12 cm/ 3 - 4 3/4 in.

1 The day before baking, finely chop sultanas, figs, candied orange and citrus peels, and almonds. Place everything in a mixing bowl, pour in water and rum, cover and marinate for 24 hours.

2 For gingerbread dough, heat honey to 80 °C (150 °F), then cool down to room temperature and knead together with two types of flour, rum, gingerbread spice and baking powder. Dissolve potash in some egg white and work into the dough. Roll dough on lightly floured surface to 3 mm/ 1/8 in thickness.

3 For the filling, crumble marzipan and confectioners' sugar between your fingers. Add egg white and cherry schnapps and combine with marzipan mixture until a soft cream forms. Preheat oven to 180 °C (350 °F), Gas mark 4.

4 Evenly spread marzipan mixture over rolled-out dough. Distribute plum preserves on top and smooth out with a spatula. Distribute soaked fruit over plum preserves and roll up dough.

5 Cut roll into 1 cm/ 1/2 in thick slices and place into greased 5 cm/ 2 in ring forms. Set onto cookie sheet on top of round wafer and bake in preheated oven for 20-30 minutes.

6 After baking turn over and allow to cool in form.

7 Melt coating chocolate, allow to cool and reheat. Cover pastries with coating chocolate and sprinkle with chopped pistachios or chocolate ornaments as desired.

Yields about 15 pastries

For the filling:
125 g/4 1/2 oz sultanas
125 g/4 1/2 oz dried figs
40 g/1 1/2 oz candied orange peel
30 g/1 oz candied citrus peel
75 g/3 oz almonds
2 tablespoons water
2 tablespoons rum
180 g/6 oz marzipan
20 g/3/4 oz confectioners' sugar
1 egg white
2 tablespoons cherry schnapps
250 g/9 oz plum preserves

For the dough:
200 g/7 oz honey
225 g/8 oz wheat flour (type 550)
75 g/3 oz rye flour
3 cl/1 fl oz rum
6 g/1/4 oz gingerbread spice - see page 26
1 teaspoon baking powder
2 g/1/4 teaspoon potash
Some egg white

Wafer rounds (Oplaten)
    5 cm/2 in Ø
150 g/5 oz bitter-sweet coating chocolate
25 g/1 oz chopped pistachios or ready-made chocolate ornaments

International Classics

Great Britain & United States

250 g/9 oz unsalted butter

330 g/11 1/2 oz sugar

2 tablespoon peel of organically
   grown orange

4 eggs

230 g/8 oz flour (type 405)

3 teaspoons baking powder

225 g/8 oz sour cream

250 ml/9 fl oz (1 cup) orange
   juice

<u>For soaking:</u>

300 ml/10 fl oz orange juice

60 g/2 1/2 oz sugar

2 star anise

4 cl/1 1/2 fl oz whiskey

Butter and flour for form

350 g/12 oz dark coating
   chocolate

<u>For sugar icing:</u>

5 egg whites

180 g/6 oz confectioners' sugar

1 tablespoon orange flavour

50 g/2 oz candied orange peel,
   chopped

40 g/1 1/2 oz coarse sugar

Christmas Cake

❶ Preheat oven to 180 °C (350 °F), Gas mark 4. Cream butter, sugar and orange peel with a hand mixer. Gradually add eggs and beat until batter is thick and foamy.

❷ Add sifted flour and baking powder, sour cream and orange juice and fold into batter using a spatula. Evenly fill batter into greased and flour-dusted springform (24 cm/ 9 1/2 in Ø). Bake in preheated oven for about 45 minutes until golden brown. Test readiness with a wooden skewer – if inserted skewer comes out clean, cake is done. Remove from form and allow to cool.

❸ Cook orange juice, sugar, star anise and whiskey until half of liquid has evaporated. Allow to cool. Cut cake bottom in half lengthwise and brush orange juice mixture onto cake bottoms. Stack the two halves on top of each other again and cover with coating chocolate at coating temperature. Allow to harden on wire rack.

❹ Beat cold egg whites in a round mixing bowl. Gradually add sifted confectioners' sugar. Distribute creamy egg white mixture into two bowls. Add orange flavour to one bowl and beat until egg white mixture thickens and clings to spoon.

❺ Pour plain white sugar icing over cake first, then distribute icing mixed with orange flavour (see photo).

❻ As a finish, sprinkle with diced candied orange peel and coarse sugar. Christmas cake tastes best fresh from the oven. Icing hardens after some time, turns brittle and loses its creamy consistency.

Ingredients for 24 cm/ 10 in springform

Angel Cake with Cranberry Jelly

❶ Combine flour, cornstarch and one third of sugar and sift three times. Beat egg whites until foamy, adding cream of tartar and salt. Combine remaining sugar and vanilla extract and gradually drizzle into egg white mixture. Continue beating until egg whites are stiff. Sift flour mixture gradually over egg white mixture and carefully fold into the batter. Preheat oven to 175 °C (330 °F), Gas mark 3 1/2.

❷ Fill dough into angel cake pan (with a smooth edge and a bottom) and bake in preheated oven for 45 - 50 minutes. Turn over onto wire rack, allow to cool, then remove cake pan.

❸ For meringue batter, cook most of the remaining sugar (leave 2 tablespoons of sugar aside) with water into a viscous syrup, this means: when rubbing a drop of this syrup between your fingers, it needs to form a soft ball.

❹ Beat egg whites until stiff, gradually adding the remaining 2 tablespoons of sugar. Cool batter by stirring constantly. Stir in honey and spread meringue batter onto cake with a spatula, shaping surface into waves.

❺ For the jelly, bring cranberry juice, sugar and spices to a boil. Soften gelatine in cold water, pat dry and dissolve in hot cranberry mixture. Pour through a sieve, onto a cookie sheet lined with cling-film, to about 1/2 cm/ 1/4 in thickness. Allow to harden and cut out different shapes, e.g. a Christmas tree, reindeer or Santa Claus. Decorate angel cake with cut-out ornaments.

Ingredients for 24 cm/ 9 1/2 in angel cake pan

100 g/4 oz flour (type 405)
40 g/1 1/2 oz cornstarch
300 g/10 1/2 oz fine sugar
12 egg whites
1 teaspoon cream of tartar
A pinch of salt
Extract of 1 vanilla bean
For icing:
200 g/7 oz sugar
60 ml/2 1/2 fl oz water
2 egg whites
1 teaspoon honey
For cranberry jelly:
500 ml/17 fl oz (2 cups) cranberry juice
40 g/1 1/2 oz sugar
1 cinnamon stick
1 star anise
2 cloves
7 sheets white gelatine

Classic Shortbread

300 g/10 1/2 oz salted butter

200 g/7 oz sugar

1 teaspoon salt

500 g/1 lb 2 oz flour (type 550)

15 g/1/2 oz unsalted butter for
   greasing of cookie sheet

1 egg yolk

30 g/1 oz fine sugar for
   sprinkling

❶ Stir together butter, sugar and salt. Sift flour, add to mixture and knead everything into a shortbread dough as fast as possible. Wrap in cling-film and refrigerate for 3 hours.

❷ Preheat oven to 190 °C (375 °F), Gas mark 5. Roll out dough and cut into 4 round bread shapes (15 cm/ 6 in Ø). Using the back of a knife, lightly score dough into rhombus shapes, so individual pieces can easily be broken off after baking. Place onto greased baking sheet, brush dough with egg yolk and sprinkle with coarse sugar. Bake in preheated oven for 20 minutes until golden brown. Remove from oven and sprinkle with fine sugar while still hot.

❸ Place on serving platter and let guests break off their own pieces of shortbread. Serve with black tea and candy sugar.

Ingredients for 4 shortbreads

Plum Pudding

250 g/9 oz veal suet

125 ml/4 1/2 fl oz milk

3 teaspoons grape juice

130 ml/4 1/2 fl oz wine brandy –
   40% alcohol

4 eggs

230 g/8 oz grated baguette

100 g/4 oz brown sugar

350 g/12 oz sultanas

100 g/4 oz chopped figs

50 g/2 oz candied citrus peel,
   chopped

30 g/1 oz flour (type 405)

1/2 teaspoon ground nutmeg

1/2 teaspoon ground cinnamon

A pinch of ground cloves

A pinch of ground mace

Salt

❶ Pass veal suet through finest setting of meat grinder. Stir with a wooden spoon until smooth and foamy. Gradually stir milk, grape juice, wine brandy and eggs into veal suet.

❷ Stir remaining ingredients into veal suet and beat into a creamy batter. Cover with foil and refrigerate for 12 hours.

❸ Fill batter into a pudding mould up to about 5 cm/ 2 in below the edge of the mould. Close mould and cover with a damp cloth. Place into a pan of water that is just about to simmer and cook for 6 - 8 hours. Store finished pudding in refrigerator for 12 - 14 days to develop its full flavour. Heat over simmering water before serving and flambé at the table if desired.

Yields about 10 portions

Bread Pudding with Candied Fruits

1 Combine whole eggs, egg yolks, sugar, milk and cream in a bowl and thoroughly beat with a hand blender. Be careful not to beat batter too foamy.

2 Cut off edges of bread and cut into 1 cm/ 1/2 in slices. Then cut slices diagonally in half to form triangles. Melt butter and honey in a pan and roast bread pieces until golden brown. Last, add lemon and orange peels and cinnamon. Layer individual slices like tiles into one large and two small buttered baking dishes.

3 Sprinkle with candied fruits and sultanas. Pour egg batter over breads and soak for 30 minutes. In the meantime, preheat oven to 160 °C (310 °F), Gas mark 2 1/2.

4 Line a deep baking pan with baking paper and fill halfway with hot water. Place bread pudding into baking pan and bake for about 1 hour. Remove from oven and allow to cool.

5 Bring apricot preserves to a boil once with some water and brush thickly onto bread pudding.

Serves 8-10

5 whole eggs

3 egg yolks

125 g/4 1/2 oz sugar

500 ml/17 fl oz (2 cups) milk

300 g/10 fl oz sweet cream

500 g/1 lb 2 oz loaf of white
   bread

100 g/4 oz unsalted butter

25 g/1 oz honey

Peel of 1/2 organically grown
   orange

Peel of 1/2 organically grown
   lemon

A pinch of ground cinnamon

25 g/1 oz candied fruits

20 g/1 oz soaked sultanas

100 g/4 oz apricot preserves

Chocolate Biscuits with Pumpkin and Ginger

❶ Beat egg whites, salt and a third of the confectioners' sugar until foamy. As soon as egg whites rise in volume and start to stiffen, add remaining confectioners' sugar.

❷ Knead marzipan and spices together. Take a small amount of the egg whites and mix with marzipan. Keep working only a small amount of egg whites into marzipan at a time, forming a smooth mixture without any lumps. Fold in remaining egg whites alternately with almonds and cocoa powder. Wrap mixture in cling-film and refrigerate overnight.

❸ For pumpkin preserves, place pumpkin, vanilla bean, cinnamon stick, orange and lemon peels, ginger, sugar and honey onto a large piece of aluminium foil and close tightly so none of the liquid will evaporate. Bake in oven at 200 °C (400 °F), Gas mark 6 for about 45 minutes. Remove spices, briefly mix pumpkin meat and pass through a sieve. Season with lemon juice and Grand Marnier to taste. Simmer until pumpkin paste has a preserve-like consistency.

❹ The following day, roll out dough to 2.5 cm/ 1 in thickness. Cut out circles of 2.5 cm/ 1 in Ø. Roll into balls between your hands and dredge in sugar. Push into deep moulds with grooved surface. Knock onto moulds to release cookies and place on cookie sheet lined with baking paper. Bake at 180 °C (350 °F), Gas mark 4 for about 15 minutes.

❺ Dip cooled cookies halfway into coating chocolate at coating temperature. Place a dollop of pumpkin preserves in the centre and decorate with two candied ginger strips. These cookies taste best fresh from the oven.

Yields about 45 cookies

6 egg whites

A pinch of salt

400 g/14 oz confectioners' sugar

200 g/7 oz marzipan

A pinch of ground cinnamon

Extract of 1/2 vanilla bean

A pinch of ground coriander

125 g/4 1/2 oz candied orange
   peel, finely chopped

500 g/1 lb 2 oz unpeeled
   almonds, finely grated

50 g/2 oz unsweetened cocoa
   powder

For pumpkin preserves:

250 g/9 oz pumpkin meat, cut
   into coarse pieces

1 vanilla bean, sliced open

A pinch of peel of organically
   grown lemon

A pinch of peel of organically
   grown orange

1 cinnamon stick

1 teaspoon freshly ground ginger

50 g/2 oz sugar

1 tablespoon honey

2 sheets unflavoured gelatine

Juice of 1/2 lemon

2 cl/1 fl oz Grand Marnier

150 g/5 oz dark coating
   chocolate at coating
   temperature

50 g/2 oz candied ginger, cut into
   stripp

Nut Muffins

100 g/4 oz unsalted butter

150 ml/5 fl oz milk

1 egg

200 g/7 oz corn flakes

2 apples, finely grated

200 g/7 oz flour (type 405)

75 g/3 oz sugar

1/2 teaspoon baking powder

A pinch of salt

50 g/2 oz chopped walnuts

50 g/2 oz chopped hazelnuts

1 Stir butter, milk, egg, grated apples and grated corn flakes together. Combine sifted flour, sugar, baking powder, salt and chopped nuts in a large mixing bowl and fold in apple mixture. Allow dough to rest for 10 minutes.

2 Preheat oven to 175 °C (330 °F), Gas mark 3 1/2. Fill 12 greased muffin cups 3/4 full with batter (muffins will rise), and bake for 20 minutes.

Muffins taste best fresh from the oven and still warm. Serve with fresh butter or peanut butter.

Yields about 30 muffins

Pumpkin Muffins

250 g/9 oz pumpkin, diced

150 ml/5 fl oz water

250 g/9 oz soft unsalted butter

200 g/7 oz brown sugar

Extract of 1 vanilla bean

A pinch of salt

A pinch of ground cinnamon

A pinch of ground nutmeg

3 eggs

375 g/13 oz flour (type 405)

1 teaspoon baking powder

100 ml/4 fl oz milk

150 g/5 oz raisins

Confectioners' sugar for dusting

46 paper baking cups
   (5 cm/2 in Ø)

1 Bring pumpkin to a boil with water, cover, reduce heat and cook until soft. Purée with a hand blender. Cream butter on highest setting of hand blender. Gradually stir in sugar, vanilla extract, salt and spices. Then gradually add eggs and puréed pumpkin. Combine flour and baking powder, sift and stir into batter alternately with milk while beating batter on medium setting. Last, add raisins.

2 Preheat oven to 180 °C (350 °F), Gas mark 4. Distribute batter into paper baking cups (double cups), place on baking sheet and bake for about 35 minutes. Allow to cool on baking sheet.

3 Before serving, cut out paper ornaments, place onto muffins, dust with confectioners' sugar and remove paper.

Yields about 24 muffins

Walnut Fondant Bars

❶ Knead sifted flour, salt, sugar and cold butter pieces into a smooth dough. Wrap in cling-film and refrigerate for 2 hours. Roll to 1.5 cm/ 1/2 - 3/4 in thickness and place into a square frame on a cookie sheet lined with baking paper. Sprinkle with sultanas and lightly press them into dough.

❷ Preheat oven to 180 °C (350 °F), Gas mark 4. Bake cake for about 20 minutes until golden brown. If necessary, cover with aluminium foil, so sultanas don't dry too much. Remove and allow to cool in square form. Decorate with walnuts.

❸ For fondant, combine butter, brown sugar, syrup and evaporated milk in a pot and slowly heat, stirring from time to time. Be careful that mixture does not get too hot.

❹ Pour fondant over baked dough decorated with walnuts and smooth out with a spatula. Allow to cool in a cold place.

❺ Pour coating chocolate at coating temperature over cake and smooth out carefully. After chocolate coating has hardened, remove frame.

❻ Dip serrated knife into hot water and cut into 2 x 5 cm/ 3/4 x 2 in long strips.

Note:
If you want to create a decorative chocolate pattern, use one part dark and one part light coating chocolate. Pour both chocolates over cake and have them run into each other. With a wooden skewer draw circles in chocolate, creating a marbling.

Yields about 26 bars

---

300 g/10 1/2 oz flour (type 405)
A pinch of salt
120 g/4 1/2 oz sugar
240 g/8 1/2 oz unsalted butter
180 g/6 oz sultanas
220 g/8 oz walnuts
For fondant:
120 g/4 1/2 oz unsalted butter
120 g/4 1/2 oz brown sugar
50 g/2 oz syrup (e.g. "Lyles Golden Syrup")
170 g/6 oz sweetened evaporated milk

250 g/9 oz dark coating chocolate at coating temperature

Macadamia and Chocolate Sweets

❶ Finely chop dark coating chocolate. Bring cream and liquid glucose to a boil. Add a dash of hot cream to coating chocolate and mix until a smooth cream forms. Gradually add remaining cream. Once truffle cream has reached room temperature, stir in soft butter and store at room temperature.

❷ For the dough, place egg yolks into boiling water and let them set. Remove with a skimmer, allow to cool and pas through a very fine sieve. Sift flour onto work surface. Make an indention in the middle and sift confectioners' sugar into indention.

❸ Knead egg yolks together with a little butter. Dice remaining butter and distribute onto flour around the indention. Place salt in the indention and thoroughly chop all ingredients with a long knife. With cold hands, rub crumbs that have formed until they have a streusel-like consistency. Then work in chopped coating chocolate and macadamia nuts. Wrap in cling-film and refrigerate, preferably overnight.

❹ The following day, preheat oven to 190 °C (375 °F), Gas mark 5. Knead dough and roll on floured surface to 3 mm/ 1/8 in thickness. Cut out any desired shapes, dipping cookie cutters into flour before cutting. Place cookies onto cookie sheet lined with baking paper and bake in preheated oven for about 15 minutes until golden brown. After baking, brush half of cookies with heated apricot preserves and sprinkle with finely chopped ginger and grated macadamia nuts.

❺ After cookies have cooled, fill truffle mixture into pastry bag with tip No. 7 and pipe onto other half of cookies. Glue together with sprinkled cookies.

Yields about 50 pieces

For truffle mixture:
400 g/14 oz dark coating chocolate
300 ml/10 fl oz sweet cream
50 g/2 oz liquid glucose
100 g/4 oz unsalted butter

For the dough:
10 egg yolks
700 g/1 1/2 lb flour (type 405)
150 g/5 oz confectioners' sugar
500 g/10 lb 2 oz sour cream butter
A pinch of salt
150 g/5 oz dark coating chocolate, chopped
200 g/7 oz chopped macadamia nuts

150 g/5 oz apricot preserves
60 g/2 1/2 oz finely chopped ginger
50 g/2 oz grated macadamia nuts

Chocolate-Chip Cookies

400 g/14 oz dark coating
   chocolate
210 g/7 1/2 oz unsalted butter
200 g/7 oz sugar
160 g/5 1/2 oz brown sugar
A pinch of salt
Extract of 1 vanilla bean
1/2 tablespoon vanilla extract
1/2 tablespoon baking powder
150 g/5 oz chopped walnuts
350 g/12 oz flour (type 405)
2 eggs

❶ Place coating chocolate into a heatproof bowl, set on top of a pan of simmering water and melt. Set bowl into another bowl filled with ice cubes and cool chocolate while stirring, until chocolate has the right consistency for piping. Immediately fill into pastry bag with tip No. 3 and pipe thin lines onto baking sheet lined with baking paper. Refrigerate, then chop into small pieces.

❷ Cream butter, brown and white sugar, salt, vanilla extract and baking powder with a hand blender. Add walnuts and knead in flour with your hands. Work in one egg at a time. Last, knead in cold chocolate pieces.

❸ Wrap dough in cling-film and refrigerate for at least 3 hours, preferably overnight.

❹ Separate dough into five pieces and, with a little flour, shape into rolls of 4 cm/ 1 1/2 Ø. Wrap dough rolls in cling-film and freeze.

❺ Take out frozen rolls, one at a time. Preheat oven to 180 °C (350 °F), Gas mark 4. Cut lightly defrosted rolls into 1 cm pieces and place on cookie sheet lined with baking paper. Leave plenty of room between cookies.

❻ Bake in preheated oven for 10 - 12 minutes. Allow to cool on baking sheet. Cookies keep for a long time if stored in cookie tins.

Yields about 50-55 cookies

Peanut Bars

❶ Sift flour, salt and baking powder into a mixing bowl. Beat egg.

❷ Cream butter, peanut butter and vanilla extract with hand mixer for 8 minutes. Add cane sugar and beat for another 4 minutes until creamy. Last, add egg and gradually work in flour mixture. Wrap in cling-film and refrigerate overnight.

❸ Thinly roll out dough to 3 mm/ 1/8 in thickness and cut into 5 equal rectangles. Layer rectangles on top of each other and sprinkle roasted and halved peanuts in between. After layering has reached 4 cm/ 1 1/2 in height, carefully roll over with rolling pin to smooth out surface. Place in freezer.

❹ Cut frozen dough into 4.5 cm/ 1 3/4 in thick strips, preferably using a sharp serrated knife. Cut individual strips into 1 cm/ 1/2 in thick slices and place onto cookie sheet lined with baking paper.

❺ Preheat oven to 185 °C (356 °F), Gas mark 4 1/2 and bake peanut bars for about 12 - 15 minutes until golden brown. Remove from oven and allow to cool. Store in airtight containers.

Yields about 80 bars

300 g/10 1/2 oz flour (type 405)
A pinch of salt
1/4 teaspoon baking powder
1 egg
100 g/4 oz unsalted butter
100 g/4 oz peanut butter
Extract of 1 vanilla bean
175 g/6 oz cane sugar
**150 g/5 oz unsalted roasted
    peanuts**

Butter Cookies with Macadamia Nuts

300 g/10 1/2 oz flour (type 405)

A pinch of salt

1/4 teaspoon baking powder

250 g/9 oz white chocolate

275 g/9 1/2 oz soft unsalted
  butter

Extract of 1 vanilla bean

175 g/6 oz brown cane sugar

1 egg

300 g/10 1/2 oz roasted pecan
  nuts

50 g/2 oz chocolate drops

❶ Sift flour, salt and baking powder into a mixing bowl. Chop chocolate into about 1/2 cm/ 1/4 in large pieces. Cream butter and vanilla extract, add sugar and beat for another 5 minutes. Stir in egg and flour mixture. Evenly work chocolate pieces and 250 g/ 9 oz pecan nuts into the dough.

❷ Preheat oven to 170 °C (325 °F), Gas mark 3. Line cookie sheets with baking paper. With a round cookie cutter of 5 cm/ 2 in Ø and a teaspoon place 1 cm/ 1/2 in high dough mounds onto cookie sheets. Leave about 5 cm/ 2 in distance between cookies. Dip cookie cutter into cold water from time to time. Chop remaining nuts and distribute over cookies with chocolate drops.

❸ Bake cookies in preheated oven for 12 - 14 minutes. Briefly leave on cookie sheet since cookies are very brittle. Cool on wire rack and store in cookie tins.

Pecan Nut Brownies

For brownie mixture:

12 eggs

1.2 kg/2 lb 12 oz sugar

A pinch of salt

510 g/1 lb 2 1/2 oz dark
  chocolate coating

750 g/1 lb 10 oz unsalted butter

510 g/1 lb 2 1/2 oz flour
  (type 405)

510 g/1 lb 2 1/2 oz coarsely
  chopped pecan nuts

For icing:

1/2 l/17 fl oz (2 cups) water

325 g/11 1/2 oz unsalted butter

100 g/4 oz dark coating hocolate

Butter for baking sheet

❶ Generously grease deep baking sheet. Cream eggs and gradually add sugar and salt. Place coating chocolate into a heatproof bowl, set on top of a pan of simmering water and melt. Beat butter until foamy, then stir in liquid chocolate. Fold hot mixture into creamed eggs. Stir in sifted flour and pecan nuts. Preheat oven to 200 °C (400 °F), Gas mark 6. Fill mixture into prepared baking sheet and bake in preheated oven for about 35 minutes.

❷ Bring water and butter to a boil and pour over finely chopped coating chocolate. Stir and brush onto cold cake. With a fork, draw lines into icing and cut cake into 4 x 4 cm/ 1 1/2 x 1 1/2 in squares.

Yields about 50 pieces each

Flavoured Meringue Clouds

4 egg whites

250 g/9 oz confectioners' sugar

30 g/1 oz cornstarch

80 g/3 oz finely ground almonds

1 tablespoon mandarin paste

1 tablespoon raspberry paste

1 tablespoon pistachio paste

❶ Cream cold egg whites in round high mixing bowl. Gradually add sifted confectioners' sugar, then cornstarch. Distribute thick, creamy egg mixture into 3 bowls.

❷ Preheat oven to 160 °C (310 °F), Gas mark 2 1/2. Mix each bowl with a different flavour paste and keep beating until egg whites are stiff. Fill batters, one after the other, into pastry bag with 1 cm/ 1/2 in Ø tip and pipe dollops onto cookie sheet lined with baking paper. Bake in preheated oven for about 15 - 20 minutes.

Note:

This batter can be piped in a variety of different shapes with different pipe tips. If you want decorative tree ornaments, garnish meringue shapes with sugar pearls before baking.

Yields about 80 meringue

Lemon Snowflakes

120 g/4 1/2 oz unsalted butter

80 g/3 oz margarine

225 g/8 oz sugar

75 ml/3 fl oz sour cream

1 egg

2 teaspoons peel of organically
   grown lemon

3/4 teaspoons baking powder

1/4 teaspoon baking soda

A pinch of salt

280 g/9 1/2 oz flour (type 405)

Coloured sugar sprinkles

Confectioners sugar for dusting

❶ Cream soft butter and margarine with sugar. Beat in sour cream, egg, lemon peel, baking powder, baking soda and salt until a homogeneous mixture forms. Fold in sifted flour with a wooden spoon. Quickly knead dough, wrap in cling-film and refrigerate for 2 hours.

❷ Heat oven to 180 °C (350 °F), Gas mark 4. Roll dough to 4 mm/ 1/6 in thickness. Cut out different shapes e.g. stars, squares and circles with a cookie cutter. Then cut out random small holes with a straw. Sprinkle with coloured sugar if desired and bake in preheated oven for 10 - 12 minutes until golden brown. Allow to cool and dust with confectioners' sugar.

Yields about 35 cookies.

International Classics

Italy & France

Panettone

1 Cover fruit with rum and allow to soak for 2 hours. Preheat oven to 150 °C (300 °F), Gas mark 2.

2 Dissolve yeast in 70 ml/ 3 fl oz lukewarm milk and stir with 100 g/ 4 oz flour into a smooth dough. Cover with a damp cloth. Turn off oven, open door and place pre-dough onto opened oven door. Allow to rise for 3 hours. Afterwards preheat oven to 150 °C (300 °F), Gas mark 2 again.

3 Knead pre-dough with 45 g/ 2 oz flour and 40 ml/ 1 1/2 fl oz milk into a smooth dough. Place onto oven door again and turn off oven. Allow to rise for 2 hours.

4 Heat 100 g/ 4 oz sugar with 70 ml/ 3 fl oz milk to room temperature, then stir in eggs.

5 Add remaining flour, egg-milk mixture, butter, salt and vanilla extract to pre-dough and knead for about 20 minutes. Then work in soaked fruit.

6 Separate dough into 2 portions and place in panettone pan lined with baking paper. Allow to rise for 2 hours until dough has doubled in volume. Cut an x in dough surface and refrigerate for 10 minutes. Preheat oven to 180 °C (350 °F), Gas mark 4.

7 Bake in preheated oven. After about 15 minutes, brush melted butter into cut and bake for about 1 hour until done.

Yields about 2 pieces

For fruit mixture:
100 g/4 oz raisins
40 g/1 1/2 oz candied orange peel, diced
40 g/1 1/2 oz candied citrus peel, diced
4 cl/1 1/2 fl oz rum

For the dough:
10 g/1/2 oz yeast
180 ml/6 fl oz milk
480 g/1 lb 1 oz flour
100 g/4 oz sugar
4 egg yolks
1 egg
A pinch of salt
100 g/4 oz soft, unsalted butter
Extract of 1 vanilla bean
Peel of 1/2 organically grown lemon
Peel of 1/2 organically grown orange
40 g/1 1/2 oz melted unsalted butter for brushing

Florentine Cookies

1 Cream soft butter, confectioners' sugar and salt. Gradually add egg whites. Combine flour and cornstarch and stir into mixture using a cooking spoon until a smooth, flexible dough forms. Fill into pastry bag with tip No. 3.

2 Draw circles of 5 cm/ 2 in Ø onto back of baking paper and place on cookie sheet. Pipe round circles onto pre-drawn circles on baking sheet and refrigerate.

3 For Florentine mixture, heat all ingredients with the exception of the almonds to 105 °C (220 °F). If you don't have a kitchen thermometer, just boil mixture for 3 minutes on high heat. Add almonds to hot mixture and allow to cool.

4 Distribute Florentine mixture inside the piped circles using a teaspoon. Press onto Florentine mixture with wet fingers to flatten cookie. Preheat oven to 180 °C (350 °F), Gas mark 4.

5 Bake cookies on middle rack in preheated oven for about 12 minutes until golden brown.

Yields about 40 cookies

75 g/3 oz unsalted butter
50 g/2 oz confectioners' sugar
A pinch of salt
1 1/2 egg whites
110 g/4 oz flour
40 g/1 1/2 oz cornstarch
For Florentines mixture:
120 g/4 1/2 oz sugar
40 g/1 1/2 oz honey
50 ml/2 fl oz sweet cream
60 g/2 1/2 oz unsalted butter
120 g/4 1/2 oz sliced almonds

Florentines

❶ Finely chop candied fruit with a large knife. Line cookie sheet with baking paper and preheat oven to 180 °C (350 °F), Gas mark 4.

❷ Slowly bring honey, liquid glucose, cream, butter and sugar to a boil, so sugar crystals dissolve. Continue cooking until mixture has reached 105 °C (220 °F, according to sugar thermometer). Remove mixture from stove and immediately stir in chopped, candied fruit. As soon as they are blended together well, fold in sliced almonds and almond sticks with a wooden spoon.

❸ Distribute mixture onto prepared cookie sheet. To distribute Florentine mixture evenly, it is recommended to use an angled spatula dipped into hot water to smooth out mixture.

❹ Bake in oven on middle rack for about 15 minutes. Florentines should darken lightly. Remove and allow to cool. Place in oven again and bake until Florentines are golden brown.

❺ Cut baked Florentine sheet into 4 x 4 cm/ 1 1/2 x 1 1/2 in squares with a large, sharp knife while still warm. Clean knife in between each cut, with a kitchen towel dipped in oil.

❻ Brush coating chocolate at coating temperature onto bottom of cooled squares or brush thinly onto baking sheet and lightly place Florentine squares on top. Allow to harden. Cut out Florentines with a warm knife or simply break away surrounding coating chocolate. If baking paper clings to Florentines, remove carefully. Store Florentines in closed containers.

Yields about 35-40 cookies

80 g/3 oz candied fruit
60 g/2 1/2 oz honey
65 g/2 1/2 oz liquid glucose
125 ml/4 1/2 oz sweet cream
100 g/4 oz unsalted butter
180 g/6 oz sugar
100 g/4 oz sliced almonds
100 g/4 oz almond sticks
1 tablespoon flour (type 405)
200 g/7 oz dark coating
chocolate at coating temperature

Walnut-Pagani

300 g/10 1/2 oz flour

1 teaspoon baking powder

150 g/5 oz ground walnuts

125 g/4 1/2 oz confectioners'
   sugar

250 g/9 oz cold unsalted butter

1 egg

A pinch of ground cinnamon

Extract of 1/2 vanilla bean

A pinch of salt

Egg yolk for brushing

Walnut halves for decorating

❶ Sift flour and baking powder onto surface, sprinkle ground walnuts on top and make an indention in the flour mound. Sift confectioners' sugar into indention. Cut cold butter into small pieces and spread onto the flour around the indention. Place egg, cinnamon, vanilla extract and salt into the middle and thoroughly chop all ingredients with a long knife. With cool hands, rub the crumbs that have formed until they have a streusel-like consistency.

❷ Push dough into a ball and wrap in cling-film. Preferably, refrigerate the dough overnight.

❸ The following day, preheat oven to 200 °C (400 °F), Gas mark 6. Knead dough briefly and roll to 3 mm/ 1/8 in thickness on floured surface. Thinly brush with egg yolk. Cut out circles, dipping cookie cutter into flour from time to time. Place walnut half on each cookie and bake in preheated oven for about 12 minutes.

Yields about 45 cookies

Walnut-Dates

150 g/5 oz finely ground walnuts

100 g/4 oz finely ground
   hazelnuts

125 g/4 1/2 oz sugar

75 g/3 oz fruit sugar

3 small eggs

3 egg whites

A pinch of salt

A pinch of peel of organically
   grown lemon

380 g/13 oz dried dates

❶ Place all ingredients with the exception of the dates into a pot and briefly roast at about 50 °C (110 °F) while stirring constantly.

❷ As soon as a homogeneous mixture has formed, remove from stove and allow to cool slightly. Preheat oven to 180 °C (350 °F), Gas mark 4. Fill mixture into pastry bag with tip No. 8. Pipe flat, longish cookies onto cookie sheet lined with baking paper and place half, pitted date on top of each cookie. Pipe remaining mixture over dates and bake in preheated oven for about 15 minutes until lightly browned.

Yields about 35 cookies

Hearts of Milan

300 g/10 1/2 oz unsalted butter

300 g/10 1/2 oz confectioners' sugar

3 small eggs

1/2 teaspoon peel of organically grown lemon

A pinch of salt

500 g/1 lb 2 oz flour (type 405)

❶ Dice medium cold, firm butter and knead together with confectioners' sugar. Gradually work in eggs, one at a time. Add lemon peel and salt. Last, rub flour and butter between your hands until dough reaches a streusel-like consistency. Distribute over floured cookie sheet, cover and refrigerate overnight.

❷ The following day, briefly knead dough and roll to 1.2 cm/ 1/2 in thickness. Roll over dough sheet with grooved rolling pin. Cut out hearts and brush with beaten egg yolk. Preheat oven to 185 °C (360 °F), Gas mark 4 1/2. Allow hearts to dry slightly, then bake in preheated oven for about 15 minutes until golden brown.

Yields about 60 cookies

Panforte di Siena

Butter and flour for mould

150 g/5 oz whole almonds, blanched and peeled

150 g/5 oz whole hazelnuts

140 g/4 3/4 oz candied orange peel, coarsely chopped

140 g/4 3/4 oz candied citrus peel, coarsely chopped

Peel of 1 organically grown lemon

1/4 teaspoon ground cinnamon

A pinch of ground coriander

A pinch of ground cloves

A pinch of ground nutmeg

60 g/2 1/2 oz flour (type 405)

170 g/6 oz sugar

250 g/9 oz honey

40 g/1 1/2 oz unsalted butter

Confectioners' sugar for dusting

❶ Generously grease springform, line bottom with baking paper, grease again and dust with flour. Mix almonds, hazelnuts, candied orange and citrus peels, lemon peel, cinnamon, coriander, cloves, nutmeg and flour thoroughly. Heat butter, sugar and honey in a pan until it reaches a temperature of 135 °C (250 °F) while stirring constantly. Pour hot liquid over almond-nut mixture, stir well with a cooking spoon and fill into springform.

❷ Preheat oven to 150 °C (300 °F), Gas mark 2. Bake cake for about 45 minutes. Allow to cool and release from form. Turn out cake onto surface generously covered with confectioners' sugar. Remove baking paper and also sprinkle the other side generously with confectioners' sugar.

Ingredients for 20 - 22 cm/ 8 in springform

Pistachio Cookies

1 Sift flour and baking powder into a bowl. Add sugar, candied orange peel, cold, diced butter, egg yolk and sour cream, and quickly knead into a smooth dough.

2 Form dough into a ball, wrap in cling-film and refrigerate for about 2 hours. Roll dough on surface to 3 mm/ 1/8 in thickness and cut out circles of 6 cm/ 2 1/2 in Ø.

3 Sprinkle with chopped pistachios, press pistachios lightly into dough and place cookies onto greased cookie sheet. Briefly refrigerate again.

4 Preheat oven to 180 °C (350 °F), Gas mark 4. Bake cookies in preheated oven for 15-18 minutes until golden brown. Remove and dust with confectioners' sugar while still warm. Allow to cool.

Yields about 80 cookies

300 g/10 1/2 oz flour

1/2 teaspoon baking powder

150 g/5 oz sugar

1/2 teaspoon peel of organically grown orange

125 g/4 1/2 oz unsalted butter

1 egg yolk

60 g/2 1/2 oz sour cream

80 g/3 oz chopped pistachios

50 g/2 oz confectioners' sugar

Madeleines

250 g/9 oz unsalted butter

6 eggs

400 g/14 oz sugar

A pinch of salt

Peel of 1/2 organically grown
lemon

Extract of 1/2 vanilla bean

A few drops of orange water

550 g/1 lb 4 oz flour (type 405)

10 g/1/2 oz baking powder

200 ml/7 fl oz lukewarm milk

Butter and flour for moulds

Cinnamon powder mixed with
confectioners' sugar for
dusting

1 Lightly brown butter in a pot and pour through a very fine sieve. Grease madeleine moulds with butter and dust with flour. Place onto cookie sheet one next to the other.

2 Place eggs, sugar and salt into a heatproof bowl, set on top of a pan of simmering water and beat with hand mixer until sugar crystals have dissolved. Remove from heat and cool mixture by beating.

3 Beat on highest setting for 5 minutes until foamy, then beat for 10 - 15 minutes on medium setting.

4 Carefully fold in flavours and sifted flour-baking powder mixture into batter with a spatula. Last, stir in milk and lightly browned butter. Fill batter into pastry bag and pipe into prepared moulds.

5 Allow to rise for 45 minutes. Preheat oven to 220 °C (425 °F), Gas mark 7. Place madeleines into preheated oven. Reduce heat to 200 °C (400 °F), Gas mark 6 after 5 minutes and bake for 10 - 12 minutes until done.

6 Turn out of moulds and allow to cool on wire rack. Dust with cinnamon sugar.

Note:
You can also coat madeleines with lemon-sugar icing and sprinkle with chopped pistachios

Yields about 30 cookies

Bûche de Noël ("Branch of Christmas")

For cherry filling:
250 g/9 oz frozen sour cherries
60 g/2 1/2 oz sugar
40 ml/1 1/2 fl oz cherry juice
A pinch of ground cinnamon
Extract of 1/2 vanilla bean
15 g/3/4 oz cream powder
2 cl/3/4 fl oz cherry schnapps

For chocolate biscuits:
5 egg yolks
80 g/3 oz sugar
5 egg whites
A pinch of salt
65 g/2 1/2 oz flour
15 g/3/4 oz cocoa powder

For cream:
4 sheets unflavoured gelatine
3 cl/1 fl oz cherry schnapps
160 g/5 1/2 oz vanilla pudding
400 g/14 oz whipped cream

400 g/14 oz fatty coating
   chocolate
Chocolate ornaments and
   chocolate truffles for
   decorating

❶ The evening before, take out cherries from freezer and defrost in a sieve overnight, catching liquid in a dish. Caramelise sugar and pour in liquid from dish and some cherry juice. Add spices. Stir cream powder and cherry schnapps together, add to cooking liquid and allow to thicken. Add cherries, cover and allow to cool, preferably overnight.

❷ Preheat oven to 220 °C (425 °F), Gas mark 7. Line 40 x 45 cm/ 16 x 18 in cookie sheet with baking paper. Beat egg yolks and 20 g/ 1 oz sugar with hand mixer until a foamy white batter forms. In a separate mixing bowl beat egg whites, remaining sugar and salt until creamy and stiff. Sift flour and combine with cocoa powder. Stir one third of stiff egg whites into egg yolk batter. Carefully fold in remaining egg whites, then evenly fold in flour mixture.

❸ Spread biscuit dough onto cookie sheet. Bake in preheated oven for 8 - 10 minutes, on middle rack. Sprinkle baked dough sheet with a small amount of sugar, cover with another sheet of baking paper and turn over. Allow to cool covered.

❹ Soak gelatine in plenty of cold water, pat dry and dissolve in heated cherry schnapps. Stir in vanilla pudding, then one third of whipped cream. Last, fold in remaining whipped cream.

❺ Spread cherry-cream onto biscuit dough with a spatula. Fill cherries into pastry bag with large tip and pipe onto whipped cream. Roll up dough from the long side. Wrap tightly into baking paper in such a way that roulade does not lose its shape. Refrigerate for at least 3 hours, preferably overnight. The following day, melt fatty coating chocolate and brush onto roulade. Decorate with chocolate ornaments and truffles as desired.

Yields about 12 - 14 pieces.

French Spice Bread

1 Line loaf pans with baking paper. Place honey, molasses and brown sugar into a heatproof bowl, set on top of a pan of simmering water and heat to 80 °C (160 °F). Then reduce temperature to 50 °C (105 °F).

2 Sift rye and wheat flours, baking powder and spices together. Mix in anise. Preheat oven to 175 °C (330 °F), Gas mark 3 1/2.

3 Whisk milk and eggs together and gradually stir into cooled sugar mixture with a hand mixer. Knead in sifted flour mixture and knead for 5 minutes with your hands. Fill in prepared loaf pans and bake in preheated oven for 40-45 minutes. Remove from oven and immediately turn out onto wire rack.

Ingredients for one 30 cm/ 12 in loaf pan or 2 smaller pans

100 g/4 oz honey
150 g/5 oz molasses
50 g/2 oz brown sugar
150 g/5 oz rye flour
150 g/5 oz wheat flour (type 405)
20 g/3/4 oz baking powder
1/2 teaspoon ground cinnamon
1/2 teaspoon ground coriander
A pinch of ground cloves
A pinch of ground nutmeg
1 teaspoon anise
125 ml/4 1/2 fl oz milk
3 small eggs

Orange Sandies

1 Cream butter. Gradually add sugar, vanilla sugar, orange peel, eggs and Cointreau and continue beating until mixture is thick and foamy. Mix in sifted flour and baking powder.

2 Fill batter into pastry bag with star tip No. 11. Pipe circles of 8 cm/ 3 in Ø onto cookie sheet lined with baking paper. Bake in oven at 180 °C (350 °F), Gas mark 4 for about 15 minutes until golden brown, and allow to cool. Dust with confectioners' sugar.

Yields about 45 cookies

175 g/6 oz soft unsalted butter
230 g/8 oz sugar
Extract of 1/2 vanilla bean
1 teaspoon peel of organically grown orange
2 cl/3/4 fl oz Cointreau
3 eggs
400 g/14 oz flour (type 405)
1 teaspoon baking powder
Confectioners' sugar for dusting

International Classics

Austria
& Switzerland

Kletzenbrot (Pear Bread)

For filling:

350 g/12 oz dried pears

160 g/5 1/2 oz dried figs

180 g/6 oz prunes

60 g/2 1/2 oz chopped almonds

80 g/ 3 oz peeled hazelnuts

Extract of 1 vanilla bean

1 cinnamon stick

3 cloves

Peel of 1 organically grown
    lemon

Peel of 1 organically grown
    orange

4 cl/1 1/2 fl oz rum

For the dough:

20 g/1 oz yeast

150 g/5 oz milk

Some sugar

A pinch of ground anise

1/2 teaspoon ground fennel

1/2 teaspoon ground coriander

1/2 teaspoon ground caraway

125 g/4 1/2 oz flour (type 405)

125 g/4 1/2 oz rye flour

20 g/1 oz gum arabic (can be

purchased in pharmacies)

100 ml/4 fl oz water

A pinch of sugar

1 Blanch dried fruit briefly in boiling water the day before baking, drain in a sieve and allow to drip-dry. Cut into coarse pieces.

2 Place fruit mixture into a mixing bowl. Add nuts and spices and cover just barely with hot water. Allow to cool, add rum and soak, preferably overnight.

3 For bread dough, dissolve yeast in a few spoons of lukewarm milk. Heat remaining milk, sugar and spices until all sugar crystals have dissolved. Combine two types of flour, add and thoroughly mix everything into a medium-firm, smooth dough. Allow to rise in a warm place for about 30 minutes.

4 Knead dough again thoroughly and work in dried fruits. Cover with a cloth and allow to rest for 15 minutes. Preheat oven to 180 °C (350 °F), Gas mark 4.

5 Shape dough into two longish or round loaves with floured hands and place onto greased baking sheet. Bake on lowest rack in preheated oven for about 1 hour.

6 Mix gum arabic with water and a pinch of sugar and bring to a boil while stirring constantly. Immediately brush onto hot breads and allow to cool on wire rack. Wrap tightly and store in a cool place.

Note:
Breads can be decorated with candied fruit and almonds, if desired. Gum arabic gives bread its typical gloss and prevents it from drying out too quickly.

Austrian Half-Moons

1 Knead marzipan, lemon juice, lemon peel and egg whites together. Work in confectioners' sugar, salt and ground almonds. Allow mixture to rest for at least 2 - 3 hours, preferably overnight.

2 Whisk egg whites until creamy, adding sifted confectioners' sugar one tablespoon at a time. Egg white icing should be creamy but not too firm. Add lemon juice. Cover icing with a damp kitchen towel.

3 Roll mixture into an 9 mm/ 1/2 in thick square and thinly spread egg white icing on top with a spatula. Cut out half-moons and place on cookie sheet lined with baking paper.

4 Allow to dry for about 30 minutes. Preheat oven to 170 °C (325 °F), Gas mark 3 and bake for about 12 minutes. Don't let cookies turn brown.

Yields about 24 cookies

250 g/9 oz marzipan

1 tablespoon lemon juice

1/2 teaspoon peel of organically
grown lemon

1/2 egg white

65 g/2 1/2 oz confectioners'
sugar

A pinch of salt

100 g/4 oz finely ground
almonds

<u>For icing:</u>

1 egg white

2 tablespoons confectioners'
sugar

1 teaspoon lemon juice

Viennese Three-Cornered Hats

1 Peel potatoes, finely grate and knead with butter, sugar, egg, sifted flour, baking powder, lemon peel and vanilla extract into a smooth dough. Wrap in cling-film and refrigerate for 1 hour.

2 Roll dough to 3 mm/ 1/8 in thickness and cut out circles of 6 cm/ 2 1/2 in Ø. Place a dollop of plum preserves in the centre, leaving a rim of about 1 cm/ 1/2 in around preserves. Pinch dough tightly together on top of plum preserves in the shape of a three-cornered hat. Preheat oven to 180 °C (350 °F), Gas mark 4.

3 Stir egg yolk and milk together, brush onto cookies and sprinkle with coarse sugar. Bake in preheated oven for about 15 minutes until golden brown.

Yields about 40 cookies

125 g/4 1/2 oz mealy potatoes,
boiled the previous day

60 g/2 1/2 oz unsalted butter

60 g/2 1/2 oz sugar

1 egg

250 g/9 oz flour (type 405)

1 teaspoon baking powder

A pinch of salt

Extract of 1/2 vanilla bean

1/2 teaspoon peel of organically
grown lemon

150 g/5 oz plum preserves

<u>For brushing:</u>

1 egg yolk

2 tablespoons milk

30 g/1 oz coarse sugar

250 g/9 oz syrup ("Lyles Golden Syrup")

250 g/9 oz sugar

250 g/9 oz cold unsalted butter

2 eggs

A pinch of ground cinnamon

A pinch of ground ginger

A pinch of ground cloves

800 g flour (type 405)

1/2 teaspoon baking powder

For butter cream:

100 ml/4 fl oz milk

30 g/1 oz sugar

2 egg yolks

1 teaspoon cornstarch

60 g/2 1/2 oz unsalted butter

20 g/1 oz confectioners' sugar

1 cl/1/2 fl oz rum

1 cl/1/2 fl oz coffee liqueur

Confectioners' sugar for dusting

Ice Stars with Rum-Butter Cream

1 Heat syrup, add sugar and dissolve. Remove from heat, add diced butter and eggs and stir smooth with a wooden spoon. Gradually add spices and flour, then baking powder and mix everything together thoroughly. Refrigerate overnight.

2 For butter cream, bring milk and sugar to a boil. Mix egg yolks and cornstarch together and stir into milk. Bring everything to a boil a few times, cover with parchment paper and allow to cool. Cream butter and confectioners' sugar and add to cooled mixture. Stir in cream, rum and coffee liqueur, and refrigerate.

3 Preheat oven to 180 °C (350 °F), Gas mark 4. Roll dough to 3 mm/ 1/8 in thickness on floured surface and cut out stars. Place onto cookie sheet lined with baking paper and bake in preheated oven for 10 minutes until golden brown. Allow to cool and stick 2 stars together as a pair with butter cream. Dust generously with confectioners' sugar.

175 g/6 oz soft unsalted butter

110 g/4 oz confectioners' sugar

Juice and peel of 1 organically grown lemon

4 egg yolks

1 whole egg

200 g/7 oz flour (type 405)

80 g/3 oz peeled almonds, ground

125 g/4 1/2 oz red currant preserves

1 egg yolk

2 tablespoons milk

A pinch of salt

A pinch of sugar

Austrian Cookie Balls

1 Cream butter and confectioners' sugar. Stir in lemon juice, lemon peel, egg yolk and whole egg. Work in sifted flour and almonds. Wrap in cling-film and refrigerate for 2 hours. Form dough into 4 ropes and shape 10 balls out of each rope. Place balls onto cookie sheet lined with baking paper. Preheat oven to 180 °C (350 °F), Gas mark 4.

2 Make an indention into each ball with the handle of a wooden spoon and place a dollop of red currant preserves into indention. Whisk together egg yolk, milk, salt and sugar and brush onto cookies. Bake in preheated oven until cookie balls come off baking paper easily.

Yields about 40 cookies each

Ischl Biscuits

❶ Cut butter into small pieces and quickly knead into a dough, with cold hands, with confectioners' sugar and vanilla sugar. Gradually work in egg yolk, salt, bitter almond oil and cinnamon. Sprinkle with flour and almonds and rub everything between your hands, similar to streusel preparation. Then quickly knead into a dough and shape into a ball. Wrap in cling-film and refrigerate overnight. The following day, briefly knead dough on floured surface and roll to 3 mm/ 1/8 in thickness. Cut out round cookies with a spiky edge and place onto cookie sheet lined with baking paper. Refrigerate for an additional 10 minutes.

❷ Preheat oven to 150 °C (300 °F), Gas mark 2. Bake cookies in preheated oven for about 15 minutes until golden brown. Remove from oven and allow to cool. Pass different preserves separately through a fine-mesh sieve. Heat apricot preserves, brush onto half of the cookies and dip in chopped almonds. Brush remaining cookies with raspberry preserves and stick 2 cookies together as a pair. Form a small piping bag out of parchment paper, fill with liquid preserves and pipe thin threads over cookies.

Yields about 35-40 cookies

140 g/5 oz soft unsalted butter
140 g/5 oz confectioners' sugar
1 tablespoon vanilla sugar
1 egg yolk
A pinch of salt
5 drops bitter almond oil
A pinch of ground cinnamon
140 g/5 oz flour (type 405)
170 g/6 oz ground almonds
100 g/4 oz apricot preserves
125 g/4 1/2 oz raspberry preserves
100 g/4 oz chopped peeled almonds
140 g/5 oz dark coating chocolate at coating temperature

Ischl Bars

❶ Cream butter, sugar and vanilla extract. Add egg yolk and gradually work sifted flour and almonds into creamy mixture. Wrap in cling-film and refrigerate for 2 hours. Roll on floured surface to 3 mm/ 1/8 in thickness and cut out rectangles of 4 x 5 cm/ 1 1/2 x 2 in. Place on cookie sheet lined with baking paper.

❷ Preheat oven to 190 °C (375 °F), Gas mark 5. Bake cookies in preheated oven for 10 - 12 minutes. Allow to cool and decorate with coating chocolate.

Yields about 35-40 cookies

190 g/7 oz soft unsalted butter
120 g/4 1/2 oz sugar
Extract of 1/2 vanilla bean
1 egg yolk
170 g/6 oz unpeeled almonds, finely chopped
250 g/9 oz flour (type 405)
For Decorating:
100 g/4 oz dark coating chocolate at coating temperature

Walnut Loops

125 g/4 1/2 oz ground walnuts

125 g/4 1/2 oz confectioners'
sugar

1 whole egg

1 egg yolk

60 g/2 1/2 oz coarsely chopped
walnuts

People all over Austria love walnuts. This recipe is simple and its taste depends solely on the first-class quality of the walnuts. Tie red ribbons around the loops and they become a favourite Christmas tree ornament.

1 Mix ground walnuts with confectioner's sugar. Stir in whole egg and egg yolk, and knead into a dough. Wrap in cling-film and refrigerate for 1 hour.

2 Preheat oven to 175 °C (330 °F), Gas mark 3 1/2. Shape dough into small rolls of 1/2 cm/ 1/4 in Ø and 10 - 12 cm/ 4 - 5 in length. Dredge in chopped walnuts and bend into loops. Place onto cookie sheet lined with baking paper and bake in preheated oven for 12 - 15 minutes.

Yields about 55 cookies

Cream Pretzels

375 g/13 oz flour (type 405)

1 teaspoon sugar

1 tablespoon vanilla sugar

125 g/4 1/2 oz thick sour cream

250 g/9 oz cold unsalted butter

Some evaporated milk for
brushing

50 g/2 oz chopped almonds

100 g/4 oz coarse sugar

1 Mound flour onto work surface, make an indention in the middle and add sugar, vanilla sugar and cream into indention. Work into a thick mixture with part of the flour. Add diced butter, cover with flour and knead all ingredients into a smooth dough, working from the middle out. Wrap in cling-film and refrigerate for 1 hour.

2 Roll dough to 1/2 cm/ 1/4 in thickness and cut into strips, 1/2 cm/ 1/4 in thick and 20 cm/ 8 in long. Shape strips into pretzels and brush top with evaporated milk. Mix almonds and coarse sugar and dredge pretzels in mixture. Preheat oven to 200 °C (400 °F), Gas mark 6. Place pretzels onto baking sheet lined with baking paper and bake in preheated oven for about 10 minutes.

Yields about 35-40 cookies

Thumbprint Linzer Cookies

150 g/5 oz cold unsalted butter

75 g/3 oz confectioners' sugar

20 g/1 oz vanilla sugar

1 egg

A pinch of salt

A pinch of ground cardamom

A pinch of ground cinnamon

A pinch of ground cloves

1 teaspoon cherry schnapps

150 g/5 oz flour (type 550)

150 g/5 oz peeled almonds, finely
   ground

Oil and flour for cookie sheet

Confectioners' sugar for dusting

125 g/4 1/2 oz red currant jelly

❶ Cut butter into small pieces and with cold hands knead into a dough with confectioners' sugar and vanilla sugar. Gradually work in egg, salt, spices and cherry schnapps.

❷ Distribute flour and almonds on top and with your hands rub into dough, similar to the preparation of streusel. Quickly knead into a dough and shape into a ball. Wrap in cling-film and refrigerate overnight.

❸ The following day, roll dough to 3 mm/ 1/8 in thickness on floured surface and cut out rosettes. Cut out small circles in the middle of about half the rosette shaped cookies. Preheat oven to 160 °C (310 °F), Gas mark 2 1/2.

❹ Place cookies onto cookie sheet lined with baking paper and refrigerate for 10 minutes.

❺ Bake in preheated oven on middle rack for about 10 minutes until golden brown. Carefully remove cookies from cookie sheet with a spatula and allow to cool.

❻ Thickly dust cookies with hole in the middle. Place dollops of red currant jelly onto the other cookies and stick ring-shaped cookies on top as a pair.

Yields about 25-30 cookies

Springerle

❶ Beat eggs and confectioners' sugar until foamy and gradually stir in flour. Wrap dough in cling-film and refrigerate for a few hours. Roll out dough without flour, preferably between 2 sheets of film. Push into springerle mould and cut out with a knife.

❷ Place onto cookie sheet lined with baking paper and sprinkled with anise and allow surface to lightly dry at room temperature for about 12 hours. Bottom side must not get dry. In case it does dry out, brush bottom with a small amount of rum or cherry schnapps. Preheat oven to 170 °C (325 °F), Gas mark 3.

❸ Bake in preheated oven for 20 - 25 minutes without heat from above. Don't let cookies get dark.

Yields about 55-60 cookies

4 eggs
500 g/1 lb 2 oz confectioners' sugar
750 g/1 lb 10 oz flour (type 405)
1 teaspoon anise

Salzburg Red Currant Clouds

❶ Beat egg whites, confectioners' sugar and cornstarch until stiff peaks form. Colour batter with food colouring if desired and fold in almonds. Fill batter into pastry bag with 1 cm/ 1/2 in Ø tip and pipe dollops onto cookie sheet lined with baking paper. Preheat oven to 175 °C (330 °F), Gas mark 3 1/2 and bake cookies for about 15 - 20 minutes.

❷ For filling, place eggs and sugar into a heatproof bowl, set on top of a pan of simmering water and beat into a creamy mixture. Remove and cool by beating constantly.

❸ Cream butter, red currant purée and cherry schnapps and fold in egg-sugar mixture. Stick 2 meringue dollops together with butter cream as a pair and place into candy cups.

Yields about 30 cookies

2 egg whites
125 g/4 1/2 oz confectioners' sugar
20 g/1 oz cornstarch
Red food colouring
60 g/2 1/2 oz almonds, finely ground
For the filling:
2 eggs
80 g/3 oz sugar
240 g/8 1/2 oz soft, unsalted butter
100 g/4 oz red currant purée
1 tablespoon cherry schnapps

Tiger Cookies

175 g/6 oz confectioners' sugar

300 g/10 1/2 oz cold unsalted
   butter

2 egg whites

A pinch of salt

1/4 teaspoon peel of organically
   grown lemon

5 drops bitter almond oil

425 g/15 oz flour (type 405)

25 g/1 oz cocoa powder

150 g/5 oz unpeeled almonds

❶ Knead sifted confectioners' sugar with diced butter. Work egg white, salt, lemon peel and bitter almond oil into the mixture. Take half of the butter mixture and work in 225 g/ 8 oz flour, rubbing mixture and flour with your hands until they have a streusel-like consistency. Mix the other half of the butter mixture with remaining flour and cocoa powder. Wrap both doughs in cling-film and refrigerate overnight.

❷ The following day, roll out individual doughs into rectangles of 3 mm/ 1/8 in thickness. Alternately layer one light over one dark dough sheet to about 4 cm/ 1 1/2 in height. Sprinkle a few whole, unpeeled almonds in between layers. Carefully roll over layered doughs once with a rolling pin to smooth out surface, then freeze.

❸ Preheat oven to 185 °C (360 °F), Gas mark 4 1/2. Cut frozen dough into 4.5 cm/ 1 3/4 in thick strips. This works best with a sharp serrated knife. Cut individual strips into 1 cm/ 1/2 in slices and place on cookie sheet lined with baking paper.

❹ Bake tiger cookies in preheated oven for 12 - 15 minutes until golden brown. Remove from oven and allow to cool. Store in airtight containers.

Yields about 45 cookies

Basler Leckerli ("Sweets from Basel")

350 g/12 oz honey

280 g/9 1/2 oz sugar

2 tablespoons water

560 g/1 lb 4 oz wheat flour
(type 550)

15 g/3/4 oz gingerbread spice –
see page 26

75 g/3 oz candied orange peel

75 g/3 oz candied citrus peel

200 g/7 oz almonds, coarsely
chopped

1 teaspoon bakers' ammonia

1/4 teaspoon potash

For spun sugar icing:

500 g/1 lb 2 oz sugar

200 ml/7 fl oz water

Extract of 1/2 vanilla bean

❶ Place honey, sugar and water into a pot. Heat until all sugar crystals have dissolved, while stirring constantly with a cooking spoon. Allow to cool, add flour and gingerbread spice and knead into a dough.

❷ Finely chop candied orange and citrus peel with a large kitchen knife and knead into dough with almonds.

❸ Dissolve bakers' ammonia in some milk, potash in some egg white. First add bakers' ammonia to dough, then potash.

❹ Preheat oven to 180 °C (350 °F), Gas mark 4. Roll dough to 5 mm/ 1/4 in thickness, the size of a cookie sheet (35 x 45 cm/ 16 x 18 in). Line cookie sheet with baking paper and place dough onto it.

❺ Prick a few holes into dough with a fork, so that the oxygen that will form during baking can evaporate and surface of dough stays smooth. Bake in oven for 20 minutes.

❻ For spun sugar icing, heat sugar and water to a temperature of 105 °C (220 °F). Stir in vanilla extract and brush spun sugar icing onto hot gingerbread sheet. Allow to cool and icing to harden.

❼ Cut gingerbread sheet into small rectangles. Store in cookie tins for at least 8 days before eating, so spice flavours can fully develop and gingerbread has turned soft and short.

Yields about 35 cookies

St-Gallener-Biberle

❶ Place honey, sugar and water into a pot. Heat until all sugar crystals have dissolved, while stirring constantly. Allow to cool, add flour and gingerbread spice and knead into a dough.

❷ Dissolve potash in egg white, bakers' ammonia in milk. Knead each leavening agent separately into dough. In case dough turns out too soft, add some more wheat flour.

❸ Roll dough to 3 mm/ 1/8 in thickness and cut into 8 x 45 cm/ 3 x 18 in strips.

❹ For the filling, knead marzipan, confectioners' sugar, lemon juice and peel into a smooth mixture and shape into 45 cm/ 18 in long, 150 g/ 5 oz heavy ropes. Place onto gingerbread strips, wrap dough around rolls and roll to a length of 60 cm/ 24 in. Refrigerate for at least 1 hour.

❺ Preheat oven to 200 °C (400 °F), Gas mark 6. Cut dough strips into trapezoid pieces, 5 cm/ 2 in on one side and 1 cm/ 1/2 in on the other. Place onto cookie sheet lined with baking paper and bake in preheated oven, preferably under heat from above, for 15 - 20 minutes.

❻ Mix gum arabic with water and sugar, bring to a boil once and brush onto hot cookies.

Yields about 45-50 cookies

500 g/1 lb 2 oz honey
100 g/4 oz sugar
4 cl/1 1/2 fl oz water
350 g/12 oz wheat flour
    (type 550)
350 g/12 oz rye flour
1 egg yolk
20 g/1 oz gingerbread spice –
    see page 26
1/2 teaspoon potash
Some egg white
1 teaspoon bakers' ammonia
75 ml/3 fl oz milk
For the filling:
1 kg/2 1/4 lb marzipan
250 g/9 oz confectioners' sugar
100 ml/4 fl oz lemon juice
Peel of 4 organically grown
    lemons
20 g/1 oz gum arabic (can be
    purchased in pharmacies)
100 ml/4 fl oz water
A pinch of sugar

International Classics

Scandinavia

Danish Apricot Stars

1 Sift flour. Distribute butter over flour in small pieces. Then add confectioners' sugar, almonds and spices. Chop with a long knife first, then knead quickly into a dough with cold hands. Wrap in cling-film and refrigerate, preferably overnight.

2 Line cookie sheet with baking paper. Preheat oven to 180 °C (350 °F), Gas mark 4. Thinly roll dough to 2-3 mm (1/8 in) thickness on floured surface and cut out stars. Place cookies onto cookie sheet and bake in preheated oven on middle rack for 10- 15 minutes until golden brown.

3 Dust one half of the stars with confectioners' sugar and brush apricot preserves on the other half. Stick 2 stars together as a pair, offset so that points of lower stars can be seen (see photo). Fill remaining preserves into a small pastry bag and pipe decorative lines over stars.

Yields about 25 cookies

300 g/10 1/2 oz flour (type 405)
200 g/7 oz unsalted butter
100 g/4 oz confectioners' sugar
80 g/3 oz finely ground almonds
A pinch of ground cloves
A pinch of ground cinnamon
A pinch of ground cardamom
Flour for rolling out dough
100 g/4 oz confectioners' sugar
    for dusting
100 g/4 oz apricot preserves for
    decorating

Kopenhagen Fruit Coins

1 Cream butter. Add sugar, vanilla extract, lemon peel, salt and eggs and beat everything until foamy. Fold in sifted flour, almonds and candied fruits with a spatula.

2 Preheat oven to 200 °C (400 °F), Gas mark 6. Line cookie sheet with baking paper and with 2 teaspoons place walnut-sized mounds of dough onto sheet, 3 cm (1 1/4 in) apart. Bake in preheated oven for about 10 minutes until golden brown and allow to cool. Decorate with white sugar icing and sprinkle with small pieces of candied fruit.

Yields about 45-50 cookies

125 g/4 1/2 oz soft butter
100 g/4 oz brown sugar
Extract from 1/2 vanilla bean
1/4 teaspoon peel of organically
    grown lemon
A pinch of salt
2 eggs
150 g/5 oz flour (type 405)
50 g/2 oz finely ground almonds
120 g/4 1/2 oz mixed candied
    fruit, finely chopped
2 tablespoons sugar icing
50 g/2 oz candied fruit

"Jödekager" - Scandinavian Almond Breads

300 g/10 1/2 oz flour (type 405)
1/2 tablespoons bakers' ammonia
80 g/3 oz finely chopped almonds
100 g/4 oz maple syrup
50 g/2 oz honey
A pinch of salt
1 tablespoon ground cinnamon
A pinch of ground cardamom
A pinch of ground cloves
A pinch of ground ginger
A pinch of ground nutmeg
200 g/7 oz unsalted butter
1 egg white
60 g/2 1/2 oz brown cane sugar

❶ Sift flour and bakers' ammonia onto work surface. Add finely chopped almonds, maple syrup, honey and spices, then place cold butter cut into small pieces on top. Knead everything into a smooth dough, wrap in cling-film and refrigerate for 2 hours.

❷ Preheat oven to 200 °C (400 °F), Gas mark 6. Roll dough to 1/2 cm (1/4 in) thickness and emboss with rolling pin wrapped with a patterned net. Cut out round cookies with 5 cm (2 in) Ø. Brush thinly with whisked egg whites and sprinkle with brown cane sugar. Place onto greased cookie sheet and bake in preheated oven for 12-15 minutes.

Yields about 45 cookies

Sweet Christmas Bread

20 g/3/4 oz fresh yeast
300 ml/10 fl oz lukewarm milk
730 g/1 lb 9 oz flour (type 405)
130 g/4 1/2 oz sugar
1 teaspoon salt
1/2 teaspoon ground cloves
1/2 teaspoon coarsely ground black pepper
30 ml/1 fl oz dark beer
170 g/6 oz syrup "Lyles Golden Sirup"
250 g/9 oz rye flour
170 g/6 oz raisins
Some liquid butter
50 ml/2 fl oz sugar water

❶ Dissolve yeast in lukewarm milk and stir in half of flour and sugar. Cover with kitchen towel and allow to rise for 30 minutes. Add remaining sugar, salt and spices. Pour in beer and syrup. Work in rye flour, raisins as well as remaining flour from pre-dough and knead firmly. Place onto floured surface and knead for an additional 10 minutes until dough is flexible.

❷ Brush with a small amount of butter, cover and allow to rise in a warm place for 1 hour. Knead dough once more and divide into 4 parts. Form into bread loaves and allow to rise on baking sheet for 45 minutes.

❸ Preheat oven to 185°C (365 °F), Gas mark 5. Bake breads for about 40 minutes. Brush with sugar water 5 minutes before breads are done. Allow to cool on wire rack and enjoy with butter.

Makes 4 breads

Göteborg Cranberry Coins

500 g/1 lb 2 oz flour (type 405)
130 g/4 1/2 oz confectioners'
 sugar
A pinch of salt
Peel of 1/2 organically grown
 lemon
Extract of 1/2 vanilla bean
330 g/11 oz cold unsalted butter
1 egg yolk
150 g/5 oz peeled, chopped
 almonds
250 g/9 oz cranberry preserves

❶ Sift flour. Distribute confectioners' sugar, salt, lemon peel, vanilla extract and diced butter over flour. With cool hands, quickly rub ingredients until they have a streusel-like consistency. Push dough into a ball, wrap in cling-film and refrigerate for 2 hours. Afterwards quickly knead dough and divide into 3 parts. Shape into rolls of 2.5 cm (1 in) Ø and refrigerate. Brush rolls with beaten egg yolk and dredge in almonds and refrigerate.

❷ Preheat oven to 180 °C (350 °F), Gas mark 4. Cut rolls into 6 mm slices. Pass cranberry preserves through a sieve and stir until smooth. Place a small dollop in the centre of each cookie and bake for 12 minutes until golden brown.

Yields about 55 cookies

Stockholm Christmas Rings

3 eggs
1 egg yolk
155 g/5 oz confectioners' sugar
250 g/9 oz soft unsalted butter
Extract of 1/2 vanilla bean
370 g/13 oz flour (type 405)
1 egg yolk for brushing
50 g/2 oz brown sugar
50 g/2 oz sugar

❶ Boil eggs for 10 minutes, rinse under cold water and peel. Remove egg yolk and pass through a fine-mesh sieve. Stir together with sifted confectioners' sugar and liquid egg yolk. First work in butter and vanilla extract, then gradually add sifted flour. Quickly knead into a smooth dough. Wrap in cling-film and refrigerate for 2 hours.

❷ Preheat oven to 190 °C (375 °F), Gas mark 5. Cut off small pieces of dough and shape into 10 cm long rolls. Pinch ends together and brush rings with beaten egg yolk. Dredge one half of the Christmas rings in brown sugar, the other half in white sugar. Bake in preheated oven for 12 minutes.

Yields about 30 cookies

Baked Decorations

Gingerbread House

Christmas is not complete without a gingerbread house. Of course, it is time-consuming, but building this colourful little house is a lot of fun, not only for children, especially considering all the delicious cut aways and sweet treats that need to be "discarded" during the building process. Once the little house is built, common consensus most of the time is, that it's too pretty to eat. Never mind - just go ahead and enjoy it. After sitting around for a few weeks it does not even come close in taste.

❶ Here's how to go about it: First, prepare gingerbread dough as described in the recipe on page 22. Allow dough to rest for at least 24 hours before using it.

❷ Make a cardboard model. Cut out a roof, a floor and windows from cardboard and try putting it all together into a model, before starting the real house made from gingerbread. Once you are satisfied with your structure, start rolling out the dough.

❸ Preheat oven to 170 °C (325 °F), Gas mark 3. Roll dough to 2 cm thickness. Place individual cardboard pieces on top of dough and cut out the shapes with a small, sharp knife. Brush different dough parts with milk and bake in preheated oven for 10-15 minutes.

4 Cool on wire rack. Stick individual building blocks together with sugar icing on a gingerbread base. Use red or white coloured sheets of gelatine for the windows.

5 As soon as house is built, you can start decorating it generously. Icicles made from pure sugar icing always look nice, some cotton batting on top of the chimney and roof tiles made from different colourful candies

6 You need about 500 g/1 lb 2 oz egg white-sugar icing – see recipe on page 36. If desired you can colour icing with different colours. You can go all out!

Note:
You need about 3 kg/6 lb 8 oz gingerbread dough for a gingerbread house. That sounds like a lot, yet you need to anticipate that pieces may break and take into consideration that the industrious builders need to check the taste of the building material from time to time. And just a reminder: gingerbread dough tastes delicious baked and unbaked.

Bake cookies at 190 °C (375 °F), Gas mark 5 for about 10 minutes until golden brown.

After cookies have cooled on wire rack, you can start decorating. You will find recipes for different sugar and chocolate icings in the chapter "Icings for Decorating" starting on page 32.

These different coloured icings can be piped onto baked cookies with a self-made pastry bag made from parchment paper.

The sky's the limit to your creativity as far as shapes and colours are concerned. Anything goes as long as you like it.

If you want to decorate your Christmas tree with cookies, it is best to use short bread cookies in different shapes.

Prepare short bread dough as described on page 24. Roll out dough as thinly as possible on floured surface and cut out cookies with different shaped cookie cutters. It is best to dip the cookie cutter into flour from time to time so that the dough does not cling to cutter.

If you want to use the cookies as decorative Christmas tree ornaments, cut a hole into the individual cookies with a straw before baking so you can later use the holes for hanging.

Besides hanging these colourful cookies on your Christmas tree as ornaments, they can also be used to decorate the table during the Christmas season. Add some other decorative items and distribute cookies over the table or on a cookie tray.

Silver pearls, small coloured balls, sprinkles in all colours or chocolate sprinkles are as much part of Christmas baking as cinnamon, chocolate and nuts. Children like all cookies. The more colourful they are, the better. You can purchase a wide variety of colourful cake decorations in stores. Be as creative as possible - you can go all out!

After cookies have been decorated to your liking, you need a suitable storage place until you are ready to eat them. Cookie tins are ideal and are the perfect storage place for a lot of variety of cookies.

Yet, freshly baked cookies taste best of all though they do increase in flavour the longer they are kept in the cookie tins.

Beautifully shaped and painted tins are also perfect wrappings for self-baked cookies to give as a present. If you want the cookies to stay moist, place an apple wedge or a piece of fresh orange peel into the cookie tin.

Index

© 2001 DuMont Buchverlag, Köln

(Dumont monte UK, London)

Conzept & Realisation:

FOOD
LOOK
KÖLN
NEW
YORK

Text und Recipes: FOOD LOOK, Köln

Translation: Barbara Sauermann, New York

Photography: FOOD LOOK, New York - Peter Medilek

With the kind assistance of :

PSL Photosysteme - Heinz Pabst, Rainer Hedkamp

Overall production: Appl, Wemding

ISBN 3-7701-7073-3

Printed in Germany

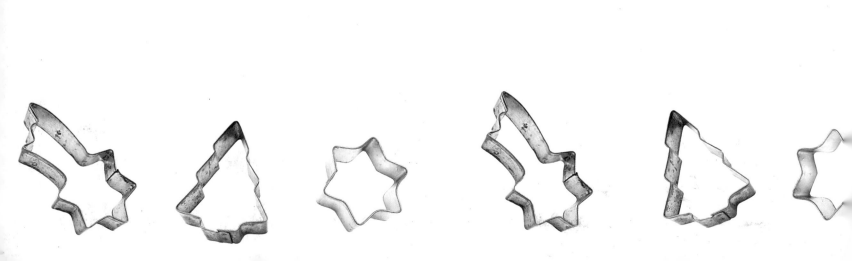